D1525849

The

CHURCH *and the*
ROMAN
EMPIRE

(301–490)

"Want to know the real early Church? Read Mike Aquilina; he makes it come alive. He is simply the best . . . period."

Matthew Leonard
Author, speaker, and founder of Next Level Catholic Academy

"In *The Church and the Roman Empire*, Mike Aquilina boldly illustrates that the early Church was the Catholic Church. The time period covered in this volume of the Reclaiming Catholic History series is one of the most important in the 2,000-year history of the Church. It was a time of theological development, an influx of Roman converts, meetings of bishops that produced orthodox statements of faith, and the collapse of the Western Roman Empire. Utilizing primary sources and constructing an engaging narrative, Aquilina succeeds in making this crucial era of Church history accessible to a large audience. This volume debunks myths and presents authentic Catholic history, as it should be: bold, engaging, and unequivocally Catholic."

Steve Weidenkopf
Author of *Timeless: A History of the Catholic Church*

"Mike Aquilina's *The Church and the Roman Empire* is a skillfully written, richly informative account of an exciting era in the emergence and development of Catholic Christianity. The story told in this volume is a compelling one, featuring heroic figures such as Emperor Constantine and St. Augustine (along with a villain or two) as well as epochal events such as the Council of Nicaea and the Church's long struggle against the heresy of Arianism that did so much to shape the faith Catholics now hold."

Russell Shaw
Author of *American Church: The Remarkable Rise, Meteoric Fall, and Uncertain Future of Catholicism in America*

"Mike Aquilina and the authors of the Reclaiming Catholic History series give today's readers—Catholic and not—an accessible and engaging place to begin their study of Church history and to embark on a lifetime journey of learning and faith."

Marcus Grodi
Founder and president of The Coming Home Network
Host of EWTN's *The Journey Home*

"Memory is the faculty that tells us who we are. Memory is what gives us our Catholic identity. Yet so much of our memory has been distorted by the falsehoods that pass for history today. This series is much needed. Every book is crystal clear, engaging, entertaining, and myth-busting. Be prepared to be surprised—and grateful for the wonders the Lord has done."

Scott Hahn
Founder of the St. Paul Center for Biblical Theology

≡ RECLAIMING CATHOLIC HISTORY ≡

The CHURCH *and the* ROMAN EMPIRE
(301–490)

Constantine, Councils, and the Fall of Rome

MIKE AQUILINA

Series Editor

Ave Maria Press AVE Notre Dame, Indiana

⧉ RECLAIMING CATHOLIC HISTORY ⧉

The history of the Catholic Church is often clouded by myth, misinformation, and missing pieces. Today there is a renewed interest in recovering the true history of the Church, correcting the record in the wake of centuries of half-truths and noble lies. Books in the Reclaiming Catholic History series, edited by Mike Aquilina and written by leading authors and historians, bring Church history to life, debunking the myths one era at a time.

The Early Church

The Church and the Roman Empire

The Church and the Dark Ages

The Church and the Middle Ages Steve Weidenkopf

The Church and the Reformation

The Church and the Age of Enlightenment

The Church Facing the Modern Age David Wagner,
Aquilina,
Papandrea

Also by Mike Aquilina

A History of the Church in 100 Objects

The Fathers of the Church: An Introduction to the First Christian Teachers

The Witness of Early Christian Women

How the Choir Converted the World

The Healing Imperative: The Early Church and the Invention of Medicine as We Know It

The Mass of the Early Christians

How Christianity Saved Civilization: And Must Do So Again

Roots of the Faith: From the Church Fathers to You

Scripture quotations are from the *Revised Standard Version of the Bible—Second Catholic Edition* (Ignatius Edition), copyright © 2006 National Council of the Churches of Christ in the United States of America. Used by permission. All rights reserved worldwide.

Founded in 1865, Ave Maria Press is a ministry of the United States Province of Holy Cross.

www.avemariapress.com

Paperback: ISBN-13 978-1-59471-789-5

E-book: ISBN-13 978-1-59471-790-1

Cover images © Getty Images.

Cover and text design by Andy Wagoner.

Printed and bound in the United States of America

Library of Congress Cataloging-in-Publication Data
Names: Aquilina, Mike, author.
Title: The Church and the Roman Empire (301-490) : Constantine, councils, and the fall of Rome / Mike Aquilina.
Description: Notre Dame, IN : Ave Maria Press, 2019. | Series: Reclaiming Catholic History ; 2 | Includes bibliographical references and index.
Identifiers: LCCN 2019016557 | ISBN 9781594717895 (pbk.)
Subjects: LCSH: Church history--Primitive and early church, ca. 30-600. | Rome--History--Empire, 30 B.C.-476 A.D. | Church and state--Rome--History.
Classification: LCC BR170 .A68 2019 | DDC 270.2--dc23
LC record available at https://lccn.loc.gov/2019016557

TO GINO,

our first grandchild

Contents

⊨ RECLAIMING CATHOLIC HISTORY ⊨
Series Introduction

"History is bunk," said the inventor Henry Ford. And he's not the only cynic to venture judgment. As long as people have been fighting wars and writing books, critics have been there to grumble because "history is what's written by the winners."

Since history has so often been corrupted by political motives, historians in recent centuries have labored to "purify" history and make it a bare science. From now on, they declared, history should record only facts, without any personal interpretation, without moralizing, without favoring any perspective at all.

It sounds like a good idea. We all want to know the facts. The problem is that it's just not possible. We cannot record history the way we tabulate results of a laboratory experiment. Why not? Because we cannot possibly record all the factors that influence a single person's actions—his genetic makeup, the personalities of his parents, the circumstances of his upbringing, the climate in his native land, the state of the economy, the anxieties of his neighbors, the popular superstitions of his time, his chronic indigestion, the weather on a particular day, the secret longings of his heart.

For any action taken in history, there is simply too much material to record, and there is so much more we do not know and can never know. Even if we were to collect data scrupulously and voluminously, we would still need to assign it relative importance. After all, was the climate more important than his genetic makeup?

But once you begin to select certain facts and leave others out—and once you begin to emphasize some details over others—you have begun to impose your own perspective, your interpretation, and your idea of the story.

Still, there is no other way to practice history honestly. When we read, or teach, or write history, we are discerning a story line. We are saying that certain events are directly related to other events. We say that events proceed in a particular manner until they reach a particular end, and that they resolve themselves in a particular way.

Every historian has to find the principle that makes sense of those events. Some choose economics, saying that all human decisions are based on the poverty or prosperity of nations and neighborhoods, the comfort or needs of a given person or population. Other historians see history as a succession of wars and diplomatic maneuvers. But if you see history this way, you are not practicing a pure science. You are using an interpretive key that you've chosen from many possibilities, but which is no less arbitrary than the one chosen in olden days, when the victors wrote the history. If you choose wars or economics, you are admitting a certain belief: that what matters most is power, wealth, and pleasure in this world. In doing so, you must assign a lesser role, for example, to the arts, to family life, and to religion.

But if there is a God—and most people believe there is—then God's view of things should not be merely incidental or personal. God's outlook should define objectivity. God's view should provide the objective meaning of history.

So how do we get God's view of history? Who can scale the heavens to bring God down? We can't, of course. But since God chose to come down and reveal himself and his purposes to us, we might be able to find what the Greek historians and philosophers despaired of ever finding—that is, the basis for a universal history.

The pagans knew that they could not have a science without universal principles. But universal principles were elusive because no one could transcend his own culture—and no one dared to question the rightness of the regime.

Not until the Bible do we encounter histories written by historical losers. God's people were regularly defeated, enslaved, oppressed, occupied, and exiled. Yet they told their story honestly, because they held themselves—and their historians—to a higher judgment, higher even than the king or the forces of the market. They looked at history in terms of God's judgment, blessings, curses, and mercy. This became their principle of selection and interpretation of events. It didn't matter so much whether the story flattered the king or the victorious armies.

The Bible's human authors saw history in terms of covenant. In the ancient world, a covenant was the sacred and legal way that people created a family bond. Marriage was a covenant, and adoption was a covenant. And God's relationship with his people was always based on a covenant.

God's plan for the kingdom of heaven uses the kingdoms of earth. And these kingdoms are engaged by God and evangelized for his purpose. Providence harnesses the road system and the political system of the Roman Empire and puts it all to use to advance the Gospel. Yet Rome, too, came in for divine judgment. If God did not spare the holy city of Jerusalem, then neither would Rome be exempted.

And so the pattern continued through all the subsequent thousands of years—through the rise and fall of the Byzantine Empire, the European empires, and into the new world order that exists for our own fleeting moment.

There's a danger, of course, in trying to discern God's perspective. We run the risk of moralizing, presuming too much, or playing the prophet. There's always a danger, too, of identifying God with one "side" or another in a given war or rivalry. Christian history, at its best, transcends these problems. We can recognize that even when pagan Persia was the most vehement enemy of Christian Byzantium, the tiny Christian minority in Persia was practicing the most pure and refined Christianity the world has seen. When God uses imperial structures to advance the Gospel, the imperial structures have no monopoly on God.

It takes a subtle, discerning, and modest hand to write truly Christian history. In studying world events, a Christian historian must strive to see God's fatherly plan for the whole human race and how it has unfolded since the first Pentecost.

Christian history tells the story not of an empire, nor of a culture, but of a family. And it is a story, not a scientific treatise. In many languages, the connection is clear. In Spanish, Portuguese, Italian, and German, for example, the same word is used for "history" as for "story": *historia, história, storia, Geschichte*. In English, we can lose sight of this and teach history as a succession of dates to be memorized and maps to be drawn. The time lines and atlases are certainly important, but they don't communicate to ordinary people why they should want to read history. Jacques Barzun complained, almost a half century ago, that history had fallen out of usefulness for ordinary people and was little read. It had fragmented into overspecialized microdisciplines, with off-putting names like "psychohistory" and "quantohistory."

The authors in this series strive to communicate history in a way that's accessible and even entertaining. They see history as true stories well told. They don't fear humor or pathos as threats to their trustworthiness. They are unabashed about their chosen perspective, but they are neither producing propaganda nor trashing tradition. The sins and errors of Christians (even Christian saints) are an important part of the grand narrative.

The Catholic Church's story is our inheritance, our legacy, our pride and joy, and our cautionary tale. We ignore the past at our peril. We cannot see the present clearly without a deep sense of Christian history.

Mike Aquilina
Reclaiming Catholic History Series Editor

Chronology for
The Church and the Roman Empire
(301–490)

378   Battle of Adrianople

379   Theodosius the Great becomes emperor

381   Council of Constantinople produces final version of Nicene
           Creed; Catholic Christianity made state religion

382   A council in Rome affirms the New Testament canon

384   Egeria's pilgrimage

386   Conversion of Augustine

387   Augustine baptized by Ambrose

393   Council of Hippo recognizes the biblical canon

395   Death of Theodosius the Great; Empire divided between
           East and West for his sons Arcadius and Honorius

397   Council of Carthage confirms Council of Hippo's canon

397–401   Augustine writes *Confessions*, his influential autobiograph-
           ical work

398   John Chrysostom becomes bishop of Constantinople

405   Jerome completes Vulgate, a complete Latin translation of
           the Bible

410   Goths sack Rome; Britain abandoned by the Empire

411–430   Augustine fights heresy with anti-Pelagian writings

413–426   Augustine writes *The City of God*

430   Siege of Hippo by Vandals; death of Augustine

431   Council of Ephesus convoked by Theodosius II to settle
           the Nestorian controversy

432   English-born Patrick begins mission to Ireland

439   Vandals take Carthage; end of Roman Africa

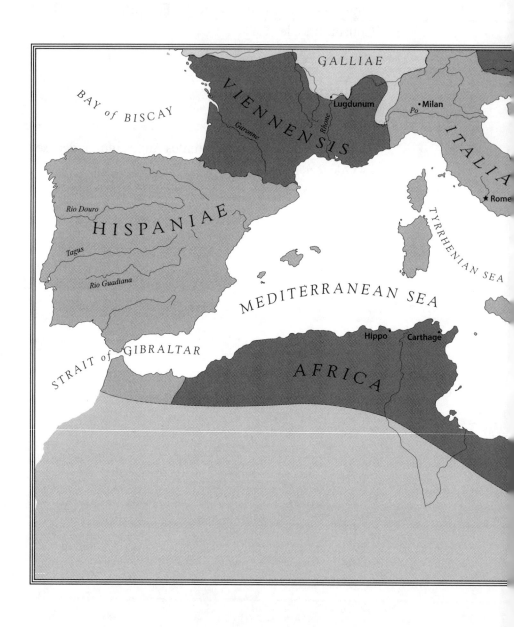

Introduction

Every era is by definition *pivotal*. It marks a turning point in the conditions of life for many people. The movement from one age to the next is usually gradual and hardly noticeable.

Some ages, however, are more pivotal than others. Some begin or end with upheaval, and people feel their effects immediately as revolutionary. This book covers such an age. It tells of events in the fourth and fifth centuries, a time when Christians moved from persecuted minority to the dominant religion in much of the Roman Empire—an empire that stretched from Britain to Syria.

For a moment that now seems brief, the Church and the Empire stood as systems of mutual support, each gradually defining its sphere of authority, influence, and power in relation to the other.

From the first through third centuries, Christians had suffered intermittent bloody persecution. Their constant prayer was for "the peace of the Church." Now, for the first time, Christians found themselves presented with what looked like the conditions for peace: the free exercise of their religion. As the Church emerged from the shadows, its scriptures took their canonical form, as did its discipline, forms of worship, and structures of governance.

Near the beginning of this era came a council, the Council of Nicaea in 325, that would ever afterward represent Christianity's mainstream belief. Catholics, Orthodox, and many Protestant bodies profess the Nicene Creed and claim the mantle of "Nicene Christianity." So important is this council that it defines not only its own time (the "Nicene Era"), but also the times immediately before and afterward. Historians call these "Ante-Nicene" and "Post-Nicene."

These centuries were a time of outsized heroes—personalities such as St. Athanasius of Alexandria, St. Jerome, and St. Augustine. Constantine the Great, the first openly Christian emperor, stands out not only in any history of the period, but any history of the world. In his own time, his uniqueness and importance were signified by a colossal statue in marble and bronze—forty feet high—in the Roman Forum. He still looms large today.

These centuries were also a time of catastrophe. Barbarians penetrated the city of Rome, sacked it, and eventually claimed it as their own.

Today, we measure ourselves as Christian by standards set by the Church in the centuries described in this book. We read the Bible that was published then. We keep the liturgy as it was set to paper then. We recite the Creed that first defined what Christians believe.

Chapter 1

The Underground

The heavy pounding at the door threw a cold silence over the little group. They had all known it was coming, but it sounded so much more like doom than they had imagined.[1]

The men looked at one another.

The pounding came again.

Without a word, one of the subdeacons stood, walked to the door, and opened it.

Soldiers poured through—maybe a dozen of them. And behind them came the governor himself. The men in the church automatically rose in the presence of such a high dignitary.

A clerk filtered through the soldiers, found himself a seat, pulled out his wax tablets and stylus, and immediately began taking notes.

"Which one of you is Dionysius?" the governor demanded.

"I am," said a gray-haired man, moving to the front of the others and deliberately meeting the governor's gaze.

"You are the so-called 'bishop'?"

"I am," the man repeated.

"Well, you know what this is about. Bring out your scriptures and anything else you have."

"We'll give you what we have here," the bishop told him. "The lectors have most of the scriptures."

"Who are these 'lectors'? Where are they?"

"They're at home. You know who they are," the bishop said a bit defiantly.

"We don't know anything of the sort," the governor insisted.

"Your office does," the bishop said. "Ask your clerk." He looked over at the clerk, who was industriously transcribing the conversation on his tablets and very carefully not smiling.

The governor also gave his clerk a glance. Then he turned back to the bishop. "Well, then, we'll leave the lectors for later, and my *clerk* will point them out. Now bring out the property."

The bishop turned to the men behind him. They had all been watching him. He gave them a nod, and they got to work.

One disappeared for a while into the back rooms and came out with a bin of flour. Another produced an armful of silver plate. Two brought out piles of robes and laid them on the floor. All the while the clerk was making a careful inventory.

After a good stack had accumulated, the men stopped, and the governor looked through it all. Then he turned to the bishop again.

"Now," he said with more of an undertone of menace in his voice than before, "bring me your scriptures."

The bishop didn't move. For a tense moment, governor and bishop stared into each other's eyes. Then one of the men turned and walked silently out of the room. A moment later he came back with a large codex, that newfangled kind of book made up of sheets in a stack bound on one edge, rather than laid side by side and rolled up in a scroll. Christians liked codices for some reason, the governor knew.

"Who are you?" the governor demanded.

"Marcus the deacon," the man replied, and the clerk noted the name on his tablet.

"This is the only scripture you have in this place?"

"Yes. The lectors have the rest."

"Your answer has been recorded," the governor said, gesturing toward the clerk. Then he directed a threatening stare at the bishop.

The bishop met it with a stare equally determined.

At last, the governor turned to his soldiers. "Gather up the confiscated property. And bring that book. We're going to pay a visit to these lectors."

There was a lot of rustling and clattering as the soldiers gathered up everything from the floor. The governor led his entourage out of the church, and the men inside could hear the procession clanking down the street into the distance.

The bishop turned to the deacon who had brought out the book, and for just a moment the two men shared a secret smile.

The Jesus Movement

We all have an image of the persecuted Christians in pagan Rome, cowering in catacombs or facing the lions in the arena. Those things did happen—sometimes. But there were long periods of peace and quiet as well. And the last period of peace was the longest one, which was what made the last persecution all the more shocking and horrible. The Church was unprepared for the persecution that ended the third century and opened the fourth. It began with the confiscation of scriptures and quickly moved to an epic scale of executions.

What made the Christians so frightening to the Roman government? After all, ancient Rome was a religious shopping mall. You had your favorite religion and I had mine, and we all got along fine together. There was even room for the Jews and their strange one-God religion. It might be strange, but it was ancient, and the Roman government respected ancient traditions. There were Jews in every city of the Empire, and as long as they stuck to their own business like decent people everywhere, they could have their private beliefs.

But Christians were different. They seemed to have come out of nowhere, and suddenly they were everywhere.

Just before Jesus left his disciples, he told them, "you shall be my witnesses in Jerusalem and in all Judea and Samaria and to the end of the earth" (Acts 1:8). The Acts of the Apostles is the history of how the apostles carried out that assignment in less than one generation. By the end of the book, the Good News has reached Rome, the heart of the great world empire whose arteries extended to the ends of the earth.

The movement started with a bang. On the first Pentecost, when the apostles took up their assignment of preaching the Good News, "about three thousand souls" came into the Way, as the Jesus movement was called in its early days (Acts 2:41). And the pace didn't slow down. The infant Church grew by thousands and tens of thousands. The growth was scary enough to attract the first persecution from the Jewish religious authorities—a persecution that scattered the believers through Judea and Samaria, spreading the Christian contagion wherever they went (Acts 8:1–4).

This rapid expansion needed organization. Jesus had left eleven men (the twelve disciples minus Judas Iscariot), with Peter at their head, to carry his message to the ends of the earth. They had replaced Judas with Matthias (Acts 1:15–26), and they ordained "deacons"—from the Greek word for "helpers"—to take care of the business of distributing charity to the poor and helpless (Acts 6:1–6). As the Church grew, it needed more "overseers"—*episkopoi*, the word from which we get our word "bishops." These were men who had the authority of the apostles in their own local churches.

As the Church spread across the Empire, the apostles wrote letters to distant congregations to give them encouragement, answer their questions, sort out their problems, and sometimes scold them if that was what they needed. It was a big deal for the congregation when one of these apostolic letters arrived. The letter was read to the whole church when they met for worship. Then it was carefully kept, and often read again. It was copied and sent to other churches in other cities. After all, that letter contained the actual words of one of the witnesses of the Resurrection, a man who had met the risen Christ face-to-face.

As the original apostles died one by one—most killed by zealous authorities of one sort or another—the men they had chosen to be bishops took their places. St. Clement of Rome, a man who had known the apostles, was one of Peter's successors as bishop of Rome. He says that the apostles knew that people would fight over the position of bishop and they therefore came up with a sure way to keep the succession legitimate:

"They appointed these bishops and then made them permanent, so that, if they should pass on, other approved men would take up their office."[2] Thus a legitimate bishop is one appointed directly by the apostles or one appointed by the ones appointed by the apostles, and so on down the chain.

The Age of Persecution Begins

Persecution was part of the Jesus movement from the beginning. The Church was founded by Christ, and Christ "suffered the extreme penalty at the hands of one of our procurators, Pontius Pilate," as the Roman historian Tacitus explained to his pagan readers.[3] Almost all the apostles died as martyrs. (John lived a long life and probably died of natural causes, and there are conflicting stories about Matthew.) St. Paul himself was, before his conversion, a ferocious persecutor of Jesus' followers who had Christian blood on his hands: "I persecuted the Church of God violently and tried to destroy it" (Gal 1:13).

But these were all local persecutions, often stirred up by mob violence (see Acts 17:5–8, 19:23–41). As yet, the Roman Empire had no official policy about Christianity, probably because the Empire had no clear idea of what Christianity was.

The first time we know of Christianity coming to the notice of the imperial government was in the year 49, when the emperor Claudius expelled the Jews from Rome because "they constantly made disturbances at the instigation of Chrestus," as the Roman historian Suetonius says in his biography of Claudius.[4] It's possible that there was a man named Chrestus causing riots, but the more likely interpretation is that the acrimonious debate over the Messiah had been causing riots among the Jews in Rome (*Chrestus* and *Christus* would have been pronounced almost the same), and Claudius, not caring what the fight was about, simply got rid of all the Jews.

That was less than two decades after the first Pentecost. By the middle 60s, people in Rome had definitely learned to distinguish Christians from other kinds of Jews. When a great fire broke out and destroyed much of the city, people blamed the crazy emperor Nero for starting it. (They may well have been right: Nero used land cleared by the fire to build his indescribably opulent palace, the Golden House.) Nero, looking for a scapegoat, seized on the Christians—"a class hated for their abominations," as Tacitus says.[5] The stunt backfired; Nero was so cruel that people started to sympathize with the detested Christians.

> Mockery of every sort was added to their deaths. Covered with the skins of beasts, they were torn by dogs and perished, or were nailed to crosses, or were doomed to the flames. These served to illuminate the night when daylight failed. Nero had thrown open his gardens for the spectacle, and was exhibiting a show in the circus, while he mingled with the people in the dress of a charioteer or drove about in a chariot. Hence, even for criminals who deserved extreme and exemplary punishment, there arose a feeling of compassion; for it was not, as it seemed, for the public good, but to glut one man's cruelty, that they were being destroyed.[6]

Among the Christians who died in this orgy of cruelty were Peter and Paul. Tradition says they died on the same day. Peter was crucified upside down; Paul, a Roman citizen, had the privilege of being beheaded.

This was the first time the government in Rome had officially decided on an anti-Christian policy. Clearly the Romans had learned that Christians were a distinct group, and clearly there were enough of them now that the mob knew what a Christian was. Otherwise, Nero wouldn't have tried to foist the blame for the fire on the Christians.

So, already about thirty years after the first Pentecost, Christians were visible enough to be targets. In the decades to come, they would grow in numbers and visibility at a surprising rate—a growth of 40 percent per decade, according to sociologist Rodney Stark.[7]

But why was Christianity spreading so fast? What did it have that people in the Mediterranean world needed?

Mr. and Mrs. Average Roman

Let's meet a typical well-off Roman couple—we'll call them Julia and Antonius. They have some money and property; they aren't exactly rich, but Antonius certainly doesn't need to work for a living. In fact, like most Roman citizens, he has an instinctive horror of useful labor. That was what slaves were for.

So Antonius and Julia really have nothing important to do. In the afternoon, Antonius might go to the arena to watch gladiators murder each other or enjoy the fun of seeing condemned criminals eaten by lions. Julia finds her own amusements while he is away: she has a couple of handsome favorites among the household slaves, and if she ever becomes bored with them, she might entice a workman off the street. Antonius knows all about his wife's recreations, and he has plenty of girlfriends and boyfriends of his own—his neighbors' wives, slaves who aren't allowed to say no, and harlots from the well-known establishment down the street.

In the evenings, husband and wife go together to parties. They start drinking when they arrive, and sometime the next morning, they wake up next to someone else's husband or wife. Then they go home to sleep off the hangover; and when it is afternoon again, they start the whole round once more.

This life of idle pleasure doesn't leave room for children—not at the moment. Julia knows several ways to make sure children don't encumber them. There are some fairly effective methods of birth control, and when these don't work there is always abortion. Or she can just carry the baby to term, if it comes to that, and then expose it—leave it out on the garbage heap, in the hands of the gods. Someday, when she can be pretty sure who the father is, Julia and Antonius hope to have a son. It would have to be a son, however, to carry on the family name and take care of them when they grow old. If it turns out to be a daughter, they'll abandon it and try again.

That is their life: an endless search for amusement. They are always looking for anything that will make the time *go away*. And somewhere in the back of Julia's mind a question begins to form: *Is this all there is?*

Oh, they are certainly among the lucky ones. They could have been slaves. As far as the law was concerned, slaves were property, not people, and the property owner could use them as he liked. He could beat them, rape them, or kill them, and there wasn't much anybody could do about it. A slave was worth something as long as he was useful to his owner; once he could no longer work, he might be thrown away like any other worn-out tool. An island in the Tiber River in Rome was a well-known dumping ground for slaves who had outlived their usefulness.[8]

And the free poor might be even worse off. At least slaves had a roof over their heads. But on every corner, in every doorway, you could find the poor—human rubbish who had no families to take care of them. And if you had no family, you were out of luck, because there was no one else willing to take care of you.

Jesus mentions one of these urban poor in a parable: a man named Lazarus who lay at the rich man's gate, "full of sores, who desired to be fed with what fell from the rich man's table; moreover the dogs came and licked his sores" (Lk 16:20–21). The picture was a familiar one in any city of the Roman Empire, and probably anywhere else in the world. Antonius sometimes had to kick one of these revolting beggars out of the way before he could get out his own front door.

So Julia knew she was lucky. But she still couldn't get rid of that nagging question: *Is this all there is?*

And then, one particularly wretched morning after, someone answered her question.

Twilight of the Gods

The first time Julia heard it, she hadn't recognized it as the answer. She asked a Christian, who didn't really answer her question, but rather told her about Jesus Christ. Christians were a bunch of slaves, workmen, and crazy people, weren't they? It wasn't even worth paying attention to what they said.

The traditional religion of Greece and Rome had a god or goddess for every occasion, but it wasn't enough. All over the Empire, rich and poor alike were looking for answers the pagan gods couldn't give them. The old gods were selfish and simple. You gave them the sacrifices they wanted, and in return they just might refrain from blighting your crops or sinking your ship. But they weren't in the business of answering questions like "Why is my life so meaningless?"

Julia actually listened to the message this time—maybe because her head hurt too much to interrupt, but it was a start. And then, later on, she was introduced to some more of these so-called Christians. They weren't at all what she expected. She didn't really know what to make of them. Some were poor and ignorant, yes, but some were rich and educated. And yet they made no distinctions; the rich and poor ate at the same tables and said the same prayers. She saw how they all banded together to take care of any one of them who needed help. She saw how they loved one another. And it seemed to Julia that she had never seen love before.

These people had found a life that had meaning, where the endless search for amusement was *not* all there was. And Julia knew she had found what she was looking for.

Her husband didn't approve.

What had happened to the woman? She used to be so much fun. Now she dressed modestly. She gave up getting drunk and sat around sober all day. And worst of all, she was trying to persuade him to join her in this weird cult. Or at least stop having fun with his friends' wives. But that was the whole point of having friends, wasn't it?

Julia felt trapped. She knew she had found the answer, but her husband wouldn't see it. She thought of divorcing him, but her well-meaning friends talked her out of it. She might yet be the instrument of his salvation, they told her.

But she finally gave up when he went on a trip without her to Alexandria. News came back through mutual friends that he was indulging in conduct that, even with all her own experience, made her blush. She couldn't share a house and a bed with a man like that anymore. She divorced him, which was quite easy under Roman law.

Antonius was furious. She had publicly embarrassed him, and he would have his revenge. He went to court and charged her with being a Christian.

Technically, that was a crime, but it wasn't often prosecuted. Rome didn't usually interfere with people's religious practices as long as they didn't make public nuisances of themselves. Paganism naturally absorbs gods from all over. The emperor Trajan had decided that Christians were not to be sought out. If they were accused, they could still avoid punishment by just making one sacrifice to the pagan gods. And no anonymous accusations were allowed. Hadrian added that anyone who made false accusations against Christians would be subject to severer penalties than the ones he planned for the accused.

Julia thought fast. When the accusation was made, she appealed to the emperor himself. As a Roman, that was her right, and it ground the whole process to a halt.

Unfortunately, some of her friends weren't so lucky. Antonius was bent on revenge of some sort. When Julia slipped out of his grasp, he made a charge against Ptolemy, the man who had introduced her to Christianity. Ptolemy apparently wasn't a citizen; the governor sent him off to be punished right away.

As Ptolemy was being led off to punishment, suddenly there was another voice raised in the courtroom:

"Why is he being convicted?"

All eyes turned to the source of the outburst, a poor workman named Lucius.

"Why are you punishing him?" Lucius went on. "He's not an adulterer. He's not a fornicator. He's not a murderer, or a thief, or a robber, or any kind of criminal. He's just a Christian. What kind of judgment is this? It's not becoming to the emperor or the Senate."

The judge stared at this Lucius until his outburst was over, and then said to him, "You seem to be a Christian, too."

"I certainly am," Lucius replied.

So the judge ordered Lucius to be taken away, too, since he had been convicted by his own confession. As Lucius gave thanks to God that he was on his way to heaven, there was another outburst, and another Christian joined Lucius and Ptolemy.

So Antonius had his revenge on three Christians. Yet somehow it looked to everyone who witnessed the scene in that courtroom as if the Christians had been the winners. The spectators walked out mumbling about how, whatever you said about Christians, you certainly couldn't call them cowards.[9]

This story is true, although I've expanded on the details, including giving names to the married couple. It comes from an account written by St. Justin Martyr, an apologist who lived and wrote in the first half of the second century—before he, too, was martyred in Rome.

The Persecution and the Plague

For most of the first two hundred years of Christianity, persecution was always a possibility, but not anywhere near a certainty. Most Christians were left alone most of the time, following the policy of Trajan and Hadrian. Once in a while there would be an accusation the courts couldn't ignore, and once in a while a mob would start a riot against the Christians, usually on account of wild rumors about cannibalism (a common misunderstanding of the Eucharist) or other strange and wicked rites. It didn't take much to get a riot going in many of the cities of the Empire, and then the local governor might decide to round up a few Christians just to placate the mob.

The stories of these heroic martyrs would keep up the Christians' enthusiasm. As the Christian writer Tertullian put it, the blood of the martyrs is the "seed" of the Church.[10] But most Christians didn't have to worry about martyrdom. They could expect to live a normal life in peace.

As the Church continued to grow in numbers, it became more sophisticated. It was still the same Church the apostles had led, but now it had more resources. Bishops began to establish permanent organizations to distribute charity to the poor members. Theologians began to tease out the meanings of the scriptures into subtle and refined philosophy. They had leisure to study the books of the Old Testament in depth, and they meditated on the gospels and the letters of Paul and the other apostles— the books Christians were already coming to know as the New Testament.

Then came Decius.

Decius was an emperor with ambition: you have to give him credit for that. He intended to solve the Christian problem once and for all. And he had a very simple plan for doing it. He would simply require everyone in the Empire, without exception, to offer a pagan sacrifice. All you had to do was report to the local commission and offer a simple libation, which was provided for you right there. Then you'd get a little certificate with your name on it saying that you had been seen making a sacrifice to the gods, signed by official witnesses.

It wasn't hard to do, and many Christians did it. "Many fell before the fight," the bishop of Carthage, Cyprian, wrote just after the persecution. "Many were laid low without meeting the enemy. They didn't even give themselves the chance to look like they weren't willing to sacrifice to the idols. They ran on their own to the marketplace. They rushed toward death of their own free will."[11] He spoke of the "death" that is worse than dying—the mortal sin of apostasy.

But there were others who refused to be part of the pagan sacrifices, even if it meant that they might be executed on the spot. And there were many who ran away into the country, choosing neither death nor sacrifice.

Cyprian himself was one of those who ran away. He was not a coward—he'd prove that a few years later. But a Christian had to balance courage with prudence. That was what Cyprian thought, anyway. However, the church in Rome, whose bishop had been killed in the first wave of persecution, sent Cyprian a rather nasty letter accusing him of deserting his flock. Cyprian explained his conduct well, though, and after his return to Carthage he was reconciled with his Roman colleagues.

But what should be done with the "lapsed"—the Christians who did sacrifice to the pagan gods but then repented? Some said they had lost their chance. They blew it. Cyprian argued differently. They shouldn't be left "to live as heathens," cut off from the Church forever, he said. But instead, "penance should be long protracted," because the sin was a very serious one.[12] Cyprian's answer was the one adopted by the church in Rome and the rest of the orthodox Catholic Church, but this question of forgiveness for the lapsed would come up again and again and lead to much contention over the next few decades.

Meanwhile, Cyprian's problems were hardly over. The persecution was still lingering when a dreadful plague broke out. "The excessive destruction of a loathsome disease invaded one house after another," one witness remembered.

> All were shuddering, fleeing, shunning the contagion, impiously throwing out their own friends, as if they could keep out death itself by keeping out the person who was doomed to die of the plague. Meanwhile there were bodies lying all over the city—well, not bodies anymore, but carcasses, demanding the pity of passers-by by the contemplation of a fate that would soon be theirs. No one cared about anything but his own cruel profit. No one trembled at the memory of a similar event. No one did unto others what he would have others do unto him.[13]

That was how the average citizen of Carthage or Alexandria faced the disaster. But Cyprian told his Christian flock that they were held to a higher standard. They had the example of Christ before them. After all, God sent his sun and showers to everyone, Christian and pagan. We should emulate his goodness.

With rousing sermons, Cyprian sent the Christians out into the streets to take care of the plague victims—not just the Christian victims but every neighbor, of every religion. And the same thing happened in other cities, wherever the plague hit. Christians poured into the streets, looking for sick people to help. The bishops organized companies of paramedics. There was no cure for the disease (it might have been smallpox making its first appearance in the Mediterranean world), but the victims could at least be made more comfortable—a cup of water, a bit of food, a damp rag to wipe their foreheads.

"And many who had thus cured others of their sicknesses, and restored them to strength, died themselves, having transferred to their own bodies the death that lay upon the others."[14] So one witness in Alexandria wrote of the Christians he witnessed in his city.

When the plague had run its course, probably millions had died. It's hard to estimate, but in many parts of the Empire as much as a third of the population might have been wiped out.

Yet in the time of plague, the Christian Church grew in absolute numbers.

It seems the Christians didn't die as often as the pagans. And the pagan sick they nursed were much more likely to survive, too. They survived—and they remembered.

They remembered that a Christian had come and risked his life to take care of them when *their own families* had abandoned them to the dogs and vultures. They remembered the difference in the way the Christians faced death—how even the dying had the certainty of a better life to come. They may also have noticed that the Christians seemed to have a much better survival rate. These were powerful arguments. Many of these pagans nursed back to health by Christians became Christians themselves.

Modern science points out that the Christians had the right idea from a medical point of view. Simple comfort care is often the difference between life and death in a disease like smallpox. A cup of water can save someone too weak to get the water himself. But it wasn't a medical idea that saved victims of the plague. It was Christian charity: the idea that every human being is made in the image of God, and that whatever we do for the least of our brethren, we do for Christ. Pagans had always run away from the sick, probably carrying the disease with them. Christians ran toward the sick—and because they were part of a community of charity, they were much more likely to save their own lives.

The Christian Church came out of the plague bigger and stronger, and now with organized charities in at least some cities that took care of not only its own members but also poor pagans who needed help.

The rest of the Empire, though, was in a mess.

Up Close and Personal:

ST. AGNES OF ROME

In imperial Rome, a young woman's identity was dependent on the men in her life—her father, her husband, her sons. For a girl to forgo marriage was to will herself into oblivion—and prolong her financial dependence on her father. Singleness was a cause for shame, and girls were usually married off by age twelve. Patriarchs arranged marriages to seal alliances between families.

Agnes had reached the marriageable age. She was strikingly beautiful, according to the conventions of her time, and she belonged to a wealthy aristocratic family. A youngish nobleman made a play for her but found himself rebuffed. Agnes, with the support of her Christian family, had already consecrated her life to Christ in virginity. She was not on the marriage market, and she never would be.

From there the story played out in the way of so many other martyr stories. Consecrated virginity, the choice for a life other than marriage, was viewed as a subversive act, a threat to the social order. The jilted man denounced Agnes before the law, and she was tried, convicted, and condemned. She was unwavering under threats of torture and refused to renounce her faith. She died a very public death by beheading, and she faced it all bravely.

Circling the Drain

Through much of the 200s—but especially after 252, the year of the plague—the imperial government was in shambles. One emperor succeeded another, only to be assassinated by the next, who might last a few months before he fell to yet another usurper. The Roman Empire was declining and falling at an alarming rate, and there seemed to be nothing anyone could do about it.

Finally, in 284, a soldier named Diocletian was proclaimed emperor, and after the usual killing of the potential rivals, he decided that the Empire needed some drastic reorganization to be stable again. He had a plan that would put an end to the constant civil wars and assassinations.

Diocletian divided the Empire into two large halves, each itself made up of two halves. An Augustus would rule over each of the two large halves, and he would pick a Caesar—some promising young man of talent—to be his associate and rule over half of his half. After a set time, the two Augusti would retire, and the Caesars would become Augusti, and then they would pick their own Caesars. It was an orderly plan of succession that simply couldn't fail.

Throughout the late 200s, the Church had been mostly at peace. Cyprian had died in a local persecution in 258, but then for a generation the Church was left alone to grow prosperous. By Diocletian's time, Christians were an accepted part of the Roman landscape. They had their own fine buildings for churches—in fact, there was one right across the street from Diocletian's palace. There were Christians in Diocletian's court, too.

None of that made much difference to Diocletian at first. He himself was a man of simple pagan religion, or perhaps superstition would be a better word, but he was more interested in the organization of the Empire than in any religious questions. But his Caesar Galerius was a fanatical pagan—maybe one of the very few genuinely fanatical pagans left. It seems likely that Galerius was the one who persuaded Diocletian that the Christians were a fly in his beautifully smooth ointment. In 303, he began announcing a series of progressively harsher edicts against the

Christians. He promised and insisted that no blood would be shed, but he soon learned that he had less control over that aspect of his government than he thought. The persecution under Diocletian would be remembered as the Great Persecution—the biggest, most comprehensive, and bloodiest of them all.

Like the persecution of Decius, the Great Persecution demanded that everyone sacrifice to the idols or face the consequences. But Diocletian also destroyed the churches the Christians had built in the long period of peace. And he decided that, to stop the spread of the Christian infection, he would demand that the Christians hand over their scriptures to be destroyed.

Diocletian seems to have watched almost helpless as his minions went at the Christians with gleeful violence, making martyrs right and left. Perhaps it made him disgusted with the whole business of being emperor. At any rate, in 305, while the persecution was still raging in most of the Empire, Diocletian stepped aside and allowed his well-oiled succession machine to swing into action.

Immediately the machine threw gears in all directions and exploded in a violent civil war. Every Caesar decided he wanted to be Augustus; every soldier thought he might try his hand at being emperor. Soon there were six Augusti rampaging through the Empire, each with an army at his command. One of them, a young man named Constantine, had been proclaimed emperor way up in Britain, just about as far away from the heart of the Empire as it was possible to be in the known world.

Meanwhile, the persecution continued. Squadrons of soldiers burst into Christian churches and houses and demanded the sacred books for burning.

Which brings us back to our friends at the beginning of this chapter— Dionysius the bishop and Marcus the deacon.

What were they smiling about?

We can imagine the governor and his crew getting back to the city hall with their pile of loot. We can imagine the soldiers carefully laying down their burdens, and we can imagine the governor picking out a few of the choicer treasures for himself. We can imagine the clerk, meanwhile, idly leafing through the big codex.

And we can imagine the look on the governor's face when his clerk tells him, "I think this is a cookbook." (Christians would sometimes turn over other books instead of the scriptures.)

Surely the execution of a highborn criminal was intended to be a deterrent. But it had the opposite effect. In fact, some historians speculate that Agnes's execution was the event that turned the tide of public opinion to favor the Christians. Agnes exemplified all the virtues the Romans claimed to prize. She was noble, beautiful, principled, and brave. Her death was the event that finally made the Romans ashamed of themselves.

Immediately upon her death, Agnes was venerated as a saint. Christians claimed that miraculous cures took place at the site of her burial. Soon after Christianity was legalized, Constantine's daughter arranged for the construction of a basilica in Agnes's honor. It still stands today.

Her literary monuments also were numerous. Many of the great intellectuals of the centuries that followed paid tribute to her: St. Ambrose of Milan, St. Jerome, St. Augustine, Prudentius, and Pope St. Damasus.

Agnes is still beloved today, and the pope observes the anniversary of her death in a special way. On that day lambs are sheared (the name Agnes means "lamb"), and their wool is used to make pallia, the distinctive garments of an archbishop.

YOU BE THE JUDGE:

Do Christians exaggerate the persecutions?

Serious histories of Christianity have never claimed that blood persecution was vast and unrelenting throughout the period before Nicaea. It's a commonplace of such histories that the periods of mass martyrdom were intermittent, sometimes carried out in brief bursts followed by years or decades of relative neglect.

But persecution continued even when the laws were not brutally enforced. Christians experienced disfavor in the courts, distrust in the military, and discrimination in many areas of life. The treatment of Christians in those first centuries can be compared to the racism suffered by African Americans in the American South between the end of the Civil War in 1865 and the passage of the Voting Rights Act in 1965. Sometimes it exploded in a rash of lynchings. Most of the time it was a pervasive and oppressive prejudice but not necessarily violent.

Christianity was a crime convenient to bring up against a hostile neighbor or a business rival in the midst of a dispute. The Christian party, a lawbreaker by definition, would hardly ever enjoy favor in a dispute.

Christians could never quite relax. The laws were still on the books. Blood persecution was a living memory within the community—and a real possibility.

Historians disagree among themselves about the numbers of Christians killed by the Romans. In the persecutions of Decius and Diocletian, the martyrs were many—certainly thousands and probably tens of thousands—as those slaughters continued over long periods in many places throughout the Roman world. But there is abundant evidence of other executions and mob murders in the years before Decius and in the years between Decius and Diocletian.

It's easy, perhaps, for some historians to dismiss as irrational the fear of Christians living two thousand years ago, to claim that they overreacted and were whiners. The victims are long dead and can't judge such claims the calumnies and injustices that they are.

Chapter 2

The Revolution

The world was, by any meaningful standard, in a mess. Emperors were rampaging across the landscape with huge armies, blighting everything in their path. Christians were being tortured, their churches burned to the ground. Disastrous military defeats in the East made it seem as if Roman power was crumbling. Drought hit the fields hard, and famine followed.

Just to add to the misery, another plague broke out, as bad as—or worse than—the one in Cyprian's time. The historian Eusebius, who lived through this age of disasters, described the predominant symptom: breaking out in great red carbuncles all over the body, and especially around the eyes, so that many survivors were left blind.

"Those who died in the cities were innumerable, and those who died in the country and villages were still more," wrote Eusebius, "so that the tax lists, which formerly included a great rural population, were almost entirely wiped out, nearly all being destroyed by famine and pestilence."

The famine had already carried off many of the poor when the plague hit. But with the plague, no class was spared. "Thus men of wealth, rulers and governors and multitudes in office, as if left by famine on purpose for the pestilence, suffered swift and speedy death."[1]

In addition to the immediate human toll, the economic cost of the pestilence was catastrophic. As much as a third of the population was wiped out: those "tax lists" Eusebius mentioned were the revenue source for the increasingly top-heavy imperial administration, and that tax burden would fall on fewer shoulders now. It was a blow from which at least the western half of the Empire would never completely recover.

But once again, in spite of the lingering persecution, which was kept up even as bodies piled up in the streets, the Christians went to work. "For

21

they alone in the midst of such ills showed their sympathy and humanity by their deeds," Eusebius wrote. "Every day some continued caring for and burying the dead (for there were multitudes who had no one to care for them). Others gathered the famine victims from all over the city and put them in one place and gave them all bread. So everyone heard about all this, and everyone glorified the God of the Christians, and—convinced by the facts themselves—confessed that they alone were truly pious and religious."[2]

Take a moment to notice what a revolutionary idea this is of what was "pious and religious." In traditional pagan religion, piety meant giving the gods whatever they wanted. But now it means protecting the most helpless of God's human creation. That idea seems obvious to us: of *course* that's what God wants. And Eusebius tells us it was obvious to pagans in the early 300s, too—but only when the Christians demonstrated it to them. There was something clearly right about Christian ethics, but it took divine revelation to make us see it.

Civil war, powerful enemies, famine, pestilence, persecution—it looked to many Christians as if the end times had come. Didn't Jesus say the day was imminent? Didn't the book of Revelation say he was coming soon? Even before the latest series of disasters, some Christians had retreated to the wilderness to live lives of fasting and prayer: first as solitary hermits, but soon in communities. With the world coming apart at the seams, more and more men and women joined them, selling all their worldly possessions and following Christ. This world was done for. It was time to concentrate on the next.

But then, when all seemed hopeless, "in the deepest darkness a light of peace shone most wonderfully upon us from God, and made it clear that God himself has always been in charge of our affairs."[3]

The Light from the West

It was a bright afternoon in Italy in the year 312. The sun was shining, the flowers were swaying in the breeze, the birds were singing in the branches, and Constantine was preparing to enter a battle he knew might be his last.

He had come a long way from cool, gray Britain, where his late father's army had proclaimed him emperor. At first, he had been content to rule the western quarter of the Empire in grudging cooperation with Maxentius, who held the rest of the West. But no one could get along with Maxentius for long.

Maxentius was a dreadful tyrant—paranoid, cruel, superstitious, and a fanatical persecutor of Christians. On the other hand, Constantine's father, Constantius Chlorus, had been the only one of the competing emperors who was friendly to the Christians. And Constantine's mother, Helena, was a Christian herself. Constantine instinctively disliked persecution, and he had better and better reasons for disliking Maxentius. For the good of Rome, for the good of the Empire, and—certainly not least— for the good of Constantine's larger ambitions, Maxentius had to go.

So Constantine had marched toward Rome.

The problem was that Maxentius had a bigger army than Constantine's and a perfect strategic position. It would take a lot to drive Maxentius out of Rome, where he had set up powerful defenses.

And what was far worse was that Maxentius used magic. No one knew what dark rituals he practiced in his court, but Constantine's superstitious soldiers had all heard of them and believed they worked. If he was honest with himself, Constantine had to admit that he was afraid of Maxentius's evil enchantments, too.

So if he was going to defeat Maxentius, Constantine needed some pretty powerful help.

He decided to pray.

But to whom? To Jove? To the Unconquered Sun? To Mars?

"God of my father," he prayed, "I beg you—I implore you—tell me who you are! Stretch out your right hand and help me in my hour of need!"

Then he turned to look toward the sun in the west. Maybe that was where he should look for help: the Unconquered Sun, the favorite deity of Roman soldiers.

But what he saw took his breath away.

Above the sun in the sky was a cross-shaped pattern of light. And with the cross, Constantine saw the words *In Hoc Signo Vinces*—"In this sign you will conquer."

Constantine ran to the nearest soldier and prodded him roughly. "Do you see that?" he asked, pointing. "Do you see that?"

The soldier looked toward the west. Then he prodded his neighbor.

One after another, Constantine's soldiers turned to face the west. And a large number of them were later willing to swear that they saw a cross of light in the sky.

Up Close and Personal:

EUSEBIUS OF CAESAREA

He is often called the "Father of Church History"—yet often, too, denied the title of "Church Father." The voluminous writings of Eusebius (ca. 260–ca. 339) are invaluable to anyone who wants to know the story of early Christianity. He lived most of his life in Caesarea Maritima, the capital of the Roman province of Palestine. While still a young man, he wrote books to demonstrate God's preparation for the Gospel not only through the oracles of the prophets and history of Israel but also through the insights of pagan philosophers. Toward the end of the third century, he began to write first a chronicle of important events since the creation of the world and then a detailed history of the Church. He quoted extensively from documents in the archives of many local churches. Today, many of these sources are extant only in Eusebius's quotations.

He lived through the ferocious persecution of the late third and early fourth centuries and was an eyewitness to the destruction of churches and execution of Christians. When peace finally came with the rise of Constantine, he was named bishop of Caesarea. He continued his researches and prolific writing.

Eusebius's role in the Arian controversy, however, has left a shadow on his reputation. His writings indicate some theological sympathy with the subordinationist doctrine of Arius—his denial that the Son is coequal and coeternal with the Father. Some of his fellow bishops denounced him as an Arian, but he prevailed when confronted, and ultimately he accepted the faith as expressed at the Council of Nicaea.

Yet Eusebius made life hard for Athanasius, opposing his methods and often calling him to make an account before synods (Athanasius consistently refused to show up, fearing a setup). It is likely that Eusebius, as a close adviser to the emperor, was responsible for at least one of Athanasius's periods of exile.

His relationship with the Church's mainstream was complicated, to say the least, and it remains so. Some commentators refuse him the title of "Church Father." Others insist that his positive contributions outweigh his scheming and maneuvering for heresy.

Freedom

"It would be hard to believe the story," wrote Eusebius years later, "if anyone else had told it. But since the victorious emperor himself declared it long afterwards to the writer of this history when he was honored with his acquaintance and society, and confirmed his statement by an oath, who could hesitate to believe his account? Especially since the testimony of later times has established its truth."[4]

That night, Constantine had a dream in which Christ appeared with that same sign of the cross and told him to use that sign in all his battles.

So when Constantine's army marched on Rome, every soldier bore a cross on his shield. To be more specific, they bore "the cross-shaped letter X with its top bent over"[5]—some version, it seems, of the Chi-Rho monogram.

And they did conquer. At the battle of Milvian Bridge (the place where this happened would be remembered for all time), Maxentius was killed, and Constantine entered Rome in triumph. He was hailed as a liberator—which of course is the smart thing to do if the winner is entering your city with an unbeatable army, but the sentiment seems to have been sincere. Maxentius had made everybody hate him. When the (mostly pagan) Senate commemorated Constantine's victory with a triumphal arch that was completed three years later, the inscription was a little vague on which divinity had granted him the victory, but it was effusive in its gratitude:

> To the emperor Caesar Flavius Constantinus,
> Maximus, Pius, Felix, Augustus,
> the Roman Senate and People dedicated this arch,
> decorated with his victories,
> because, by the prompting of the Divinity,
> by the greatness of his mind,
> he, with his army, in one moment by a just victory
> avenged the state both on the tyrant and on all his party.

This arch still stands today in Rome. There are no Christian symbols on it at all, probably for at least two reasons. One was that, although there were many Christians in Rome, the conservative Senate still clung to pagan traditions, and would cling to them for decades afterward. The other was that most of the sculptures on the arch were pillaged from older monuments. It may well be that, after decades of disasters—civil wars, freak storms, droughts, famines, persecutions, and above all the devastating plagues—there simply weren't any artists left who could do work that the Senate (or Constantine himself) considered good enough.

Constantine's victory changed everything. It liberated Rome from a dreadful tyrant. It put Constantine in control of the western half of the Roman Empire. And it ended the persecution of the Christians in the West. It must have seemed as if the world had turned upside down.

But even the most optimistic Christian might not have predicted what happened the next year.

In 313, Constantine and the remaining Eastern emperor, Licinius, met at Milan, a city rapidly growing into the new metropolis of Italy. Technically they were coequal Augusti, but it seemed pretty clear that Constantine was the one with the real power. So the famous edict the two issued at Milan was probably Constantine's idea. Licinius most likely signed it to remain on Constantine's good side.

"Our purpose," the emperors wrote to their governors, "is to grant to the Christians and to all others full authority to follow whatever worship each man has desired, whereby whatsoever Divinity dwells in heaven may be benevolent and propitious to us and to all who are placed under our authority. Therefore we thought it salutary and most proper to establish our purpose that no man whatever should be refused complete toleration, who has given up his mind either to the cult of the Christians or to the religion which he personally feels best suited to himself, to the end that the supreme Divinity, to whose worship we devote ourselves under no compulsion, may continue in all things to grant us his usual favor and benevolence."

This was a bombshell. It wasn't just that Christianity would be tolerated. That had happened before as the temporary whim of an emperor, expressed as an act of imperial benevolence. Here the toleration was expressed as a legal principle. And although the Edict of Milan specifically mentioned Christians, the letter from the emperors made it very clear that Christians weren't the only ones to benefit. "And when you perceive that we have granted this favor to the said Christians, your Devotedness understands that to others also freedom for their own worship and cult is likewise left open and freely granted, as befits the quiet of our times, that every man may have complete toleration in the practice of whatever worship he has chosen."[6]

For the first time in history, complete religious freedom was the law of a great world power. The *only* great world power. Christians rejoiced, liberty reigned, and everyone lived happily ever after.

And if that were true, our story would end here. But it turns out that freedom is a lot more complicated than it sounds.

Which Church Is *the* Church?

When Constantine and the probably reluctant Licinius issued their Edict of Milan, one of the things they took care of was restoring property that had been confiscated from Christians during the Great Persecution. Anyone who had received confiscated property must return it to the Christian owners—either individuals or the Church—"without payment or price."

Of course, Constantine understood that some people might have bought those properties in good faith, since it was legally confiscated, so the edict specified that "those who restore them without price, as we said, shall expect a compensation from our benevolence."

There. That was simple. Everything sorted out, everyone happy.

Constantine wrote letters to the governors instructing them to make the proper restorations immediately. For example, he wrote to the proconsul of Africa that "if any of those things that belonged to the Catholic Church of the Christians in any city, or even in other places, are now in the possession either of citizens or of any others, you should have them restored immediately to these same churches, since it has been our determination that those things which these same churches possessed before should be restored to them as their right."[7]

Constantine also gave the Catholic clergy the same privileges the pagan priests had—most notably that they should be "absolutely free from all the public offices," which were becoming more and more of a burden to the officeholders. He obviously had no idea what effect this policy would have, but he would soon find out as officials responsible for the increasingly heavy imperial taxes flocked to the clergy.

Aside from restoring property and granting privileges to the Church, Constantine also made large donations. He wrote to Caecilian, bishop of Carthage in the African province of Numidia, that he had instructed his government to hand over a big pile of cash to the "ministers of the lawful and most holy Catholic religion."[8]

That letter was sent to Caecilian through the governor Anulinus, who reported that he had forwarded it as instructed. "But a few days later," he continued, "I was approached by certain persons, followed by a great throng of the populace, who held that Caecilian must be opposed, and presented me in my official capacity with two documents (one bound in leather and sealed, the other an unsealed document), and demanded insistently that I should send them to the sacred and venerable court of your Highness."[9]

Constantine had both documents before him as he read Anulinus's letter. The sealed one bound in leather had a label:

STATEMENT OF THE CATHOLIC CHURCH
OF CHARGES AGAINST CAECILIAN
DELIVERED BY THE PARTY OF MAJORINUS

The unsealed document was a petition urging Constantine to appoint judges from Gaul—neutral territory far from Africa—because "between us and other bishops in Africa disputes have arisen." And it was signed by "Lucianus, Dignus, Nasutius, Capito, Fidentius, and the rest of the bishops who adhere to Donatus."[10]

What was this? The "Catholic Church" making charges against the bishop of Carthage? Who was this Majorinus? And what did the petitioners mean by "bishops who adhere to Donatus"?

All Constantine wanted to do was give the Catholic Church in Africa what belonged to it, and a nice little gift besides. Now he was going to have to figure out *who* the Catholic Church was.

He wrote to the bishop of Rome that "it seems to me to be a very serious matter that in those provinces which Divine Providence has chosen to entrust to my Devotedness, and where there is a large population, the multitude should be found pursuing the worse course of action, spitting up, as it were, and the bishops at variance among themselves."[11] So he brought Caecilian and his accusers to Rome, where the requested bishops from Gaul heard the accusations and judged Caecilian innocent. And that should have been the end of it.

It wasn't the end of it, though. The "Donatists"—the bishops who adhered to Donatus—demanded a council to settle the issue. Constantine called a council at Arles in Gaul, and again the decision was in favor of Caecilian. But the Donatist party still wouldn't accept it.

Constantine had stumbled on a deep rift in the local church in Africa, and it gave him a quick education in how hard it could be to deal with the Holy Catholic Church. Especially now that the Church was basking in the light of imperial favor, there were all sorts of little groups claiming to be the only true Church.

This was nothing new, of course. The apostle John had to deal with baseless accusations from someone named Diotrephes (see 3 Jn 9–10). Paul often warned against teachers who brought a "different doctrine" (1 Tm 1:3). Aside from the mainstream Church, there had always been a variety of small sects who claimed to have the true teaching of Christ. What was different was that there was now an emperor who was willing to be lavishly generous to the Holy Catholic Church, which gave some of the smaller sects a strong motivation to put on the mask of the larger organization.

The Donatists were one of the biggest, and even they were a small (but troublesome) minority. They accused their opponents of having been *traditores*—people who "handed over" the scriptures to be destroyed during the Great Persecution. (*Traditor*, incidentally, is the word that gives us our English *traitor*.) They also thought that the mainstream Church was far too lenient on the Christians who had lapsed and made pagan sacrifices during the persecution—the same old argument Cyprian had dealt with during the Decian persecution. They had rejected Caecilian and appointed a counterbishop of their own, Majorinus.

Once Constantine had decided that Caecilian's was the real Catholic Church, it necessarily followed that the confiscated property and the imperial donations belonged to that group and not to the Donatists. Thus Constantine found himself in the awkward position of having to turn the law on a group of Christians. And of course the Donatists portrayed him as a persecutor.

As time went on, the Donatists proved ready to use fraud and violence to get their way. Other malcontents attached themselves to the cause, and even a terrorist movement associated with Donatists plagued Roman Africa for decades.

This was not at all what Constantine had envisioned when he took up the Christian cause. The Donatist schism, he said, "gives an opportunity of detraction to those who are known to turn their minds away from the keeping of the most holy Catholic law." He wouldn't stop worrying until "all, bound together in brotherly concord, adore the most holy God with the worship of the Catholic religion that is his due."[12] That was his picture of the ideal Christian empire, and it was very frustrating to Constantine when Christians kept getting in the way of it.

After a while of trying to sort out the Donatist schism, Constantine gave up and frankly told the African bishops they would have to put up with the Donatist nuisance. He may have realized that he would soon have bigger problems to deal with. It was becoming more and more clear that Licinius would have to go. Licinius was showing his true stripes, turning into a persecuting pagan bigot, and there was no room for that sort of thing in Constantine's empire.

Christianizing the World

The Donatist schism was a sideshow. The main attraction was still the incredible rise of the Christian faith from persecuted underground cult to "the lawful and most holy Catholic religion."

Magnificent churches sprang up in cities everywhere. Most were built in the basilica form commonly used for Roman public buildings. They were rectangular and oblong, with a semicircular apse at one end. Many grand civic basilicas (courthouses and gathering places) were converted to sacred use. Constantine himself donated a fine basilica over the tomb of St. Peter in Rome, one that would stand for more than a thousand years until it was finally replaced by the current St. Peter's. His mother Helena made a pilgrimage to Judea to see the holy places where Christ himself had trod. She supervised what might have been the world's first organized archaeological dig to find the tomb where Christ had lain—a tomb that had been deliberately obscured by a pagan temple in the reign of Hadrian. There she found what she believed—and it was confirmed by a miracle—to be the True Cross, the Cross on which Jesus had died. It was carefully preserved as a holy relic and became Constantine's most prized imperial possession.

The world was beginning to look more Christian than pagan. Christian bishops were now in honored positions of trust as advisers to the emperor and his governor; Christians walked through the streets without looking over their shoulders and appeared in public in their Sunday best. Pilgrims began to flock to the holy sites in Judea, following the example of Helena, and Constantine made sure there were grand churches for them to worship in once they got there. Even the law was beginning to look a bit more Christian. Constantine decreed protections for slaves, for example, that actually punished a slave owner for murdering his property.

Aside from the Donatist unpleasantness, it was a great time for the Christian Church. And then an obscure priest named Arius came along and threw the whole world into an uproar.

YOU BE THE JUDGE:

Did Constantine force Christianity on unwilling pagans?

No. One of his successors later in the fourth century, Theodosius, did enact coercive legal measures to eradicate paganism. But Constantine abhorred that kind of action.

One of Constantine's court intellectuals, a Christian named Lactantius, wrote eloquently in defense of religious freedom. He may have been an important influence in shaping the young emperor's understanding of conscience: "Torture and piety are quite different things," he wrote. "Truth cannot be joined to force or justice to cruelty"(Lactantius, *Divine Institutes* 5.19).

Constantine's Edict of Milan did not favor Christianity over any other religion. It simply granted Christians the status already enjoyed by other cults—so that "each one may have the free opportunity to worship as he pleases; this regulation is made that we may not seem to detract from any dignity of any religion."

Constantine's later edicts—to the Palestinians and to the Eastern provincials—show even more mature doctrine, put sometimes in poetic terms: "Let no one disturb another. Let each man hold fast to that which his soul wishes. Let him make full use of this."

Some novelists mistakenly try to smear Constantine as a religious zealot and tyrant. Quite the opposite is true. He was the first imperial champion of religious freedom and tolerance.

Chapter 3

Nicaea

Five years after the Edict of Milan, the church in Alexandria was flourishing. The number of Christians was growing every year, and the sermons of Bishop Alexander attracted big crowds at the biggest church in the city. One day Alexander decided to preach on the subject of Father, Son, and Holy Spirit: how God can be one, and yet also three.

The sermon got people talking. And one of the people who started talking was one of Alexander's own priests, a man named Arius. He was an obscure unknown, but he had opinions. And in his opinion, Alexander had it all wrong.

We don't know exactly what Alexander said. The text of his sermon hasn't survived. But he obviously said something about what the Church had always believed: that the Son is eternally God, as the Father is eternally God.

And Arius jumped on it.

Arius was above all a logician, and he saw a logical flaw in what Alexander preached. "If the Father begot the Son," he said, "then the one who was begotten began to exist. And from that it is clear that there was a time when the Son was not."[1]

Alexander heard what Arius said, and reacted the way you might expect someone to react who has always been an orthodox Christian:

"What?"

Arius

But who was this Arius? Where did he come from, and what made him think he could turn Christian theology upside down?

We don't know all that much about Arius, and it's important to remember that most of what we think we know comes from Arius's enemies. So we have to be careful about how seriously we take the information that's available. Still, we have a few details, and a little of Arius's own writing. And we can judge a little of his character from the character of his ideas.

Arius was a priest in Alexandria, and just that location tells us something. Alexandria, the capital of Roman Egypt, was a city mad for debates. It was the intellectual capital of the Mediterranean world. Its famous library supposedly held a copy (or the original manuscript) of every book ever written. Students came to the city from all over the Empire for a graduate education in philosophy, mathematics, medicine, astronomy, or—especially—rhetoric. It had built itself into a city of debaters, and it wasn't uncommon at all for the debates to turn into riots.

In a city where debating was what got you noticed, Arius had the right equipment. Everyone agreed that he was skilled in logic: "a man possessed of no inconsiderable logical acumen," the historian Socrates (not to be confused with the philosopher) called him;[2] and Sozomen, another church historian, said that Arius was "a most expert logician, for he is said to have been not without proficiency even in such studies."[3]

Arius was an enthusiastic Christian, but an even more enthusiastic debater. He loved a good fight, as long as it was a fight with words. We first hear of him as one of the followers of Melitius, an ambitious bishop during the Great Persecution who put himself in charge and tried to take over both the priests and the charity workers while Peter, the bishop of Alexandria, was in prison, even though Peter had set up a system of parish visitors to administer the diocese in his absence. But Arius left the party of Melitius and was ordained a deacon by Peter. Then he quarreled with Peter when Peter excommunicated Melitius, and he did it publicly enough—"he couldn't bear to keep quiet," Sozomen says[4]—that Peter ended up excommunicating Arius as well. But after Peter was martyred, Arius switched sides again and was ordained a priest by Peter's successor Achillas. Achillas's successor, Alexander, recognized Arius's talents—but then came the disagreement over the nature of Christ encapsulated by Arius's slogan: "There was a time when he was not."

This short biography (and, short though it is, it's just about everything we know about Arius up to his outburst) gives us a consistent portrait of Arius's personality. He seems to have disagreed for the sake of disagreeing. If we count his initial switch to Melitius's party, he switched sides four times in the Melitian schism. And he was just getting warmed up.

Alexander was a modest and charitable Christian. He did nothing in haste. In fact, Sozomen says, "some who heard these doctrines blamed Alexander because he ought not to put up with novelties at variance with the faith."[5] But Alexander thought it would be best to have Arius state his views and some of the other clergy argue against him. Then Alexander could make a decision after due consideration. So he set up a kind of trial, and Arius had a chance to explain what he believed.[6]

What did he believe? "God was not always a Father," he told anyone who would listen. "There was a time when he was not a Father. The Word of God did not exist from eternity, but was made out of nothing." Thus Arius's catchphrase: "There was a time when he was not." God made the Son, he said; "the Son is a creature and a work." And that meant that "he is by nature mutable and susceptible of change, as all other rational things are. Hence the Word is alien to, foreign to, and excluded from the essence of God. And the Father is invisible to the Son, for the Son does not perfectly and accurately know the Father, nor can he perfectly behold him." The Father made the Son first in order to create us through him; he was a sort of tool of creation.

All this sounded very shocking to the priests Alexander had brought to argue the other side. The Son a creature? Susceptible to change?

"Do you mean," they asked Arius, "that, since the Son is a creature, he could change from good to evil the way the devil did?"

They were pretty sure they had him there.

But Arius said that was exactly what he meant. The Son was a creature, and creatures can change. He *didn't* change, but he *could*.[7]

That answer probably caused a bit of an outburst from the other side. But eventually they calmed down and presented their case. The Son, they said, was not a creature. He was of the same being as the Father, coeternal with the Father.[8] This was what Christians had always believed.

Smugly confident of his logic, Arius insisted that they were being irrational. If they would just think logically . . .

But in the end Alexander had no trouble deciding against Arius.

From Arius to Arianism

And that might have been the end of it. Arius was stubborn, but he was just one priest. Alexander was still the bishop, and he had the authority to excommunicate Arius if he had to.

But there was another ambitious bishop who suddenly stepped in, even though it wasn't his business at all. His name was Eusebius—a very common name in those days. We know him as Eusebius of Nicomedia, to distinguish him from other Eusebiuses like Eusebius of Caesarea, the famous historian.

He was "of Nicomedia," which was the imperial capital of the East at the time, because he had wangled an appointment there even though he was already bishop of Berytus, and the rule back then was that a bishop couldn't change his diocese. It was, the argument ran, like a husband deserting his wife. We don't know why Eusebius decided to meddle in the Arius affair across the sea in Alexandria, but meddle he did. It was enough to make even the gentle and charitable Bishop Alexander grumpy and sarcastic.

"I really wanted to leave this mess in silence," he wrote in an encyclical letter to the other bishops,

> to keep it—if possible—confined only to its supporters, so it wouldn't go out into other districts and poison the ears of some of the simple. But since Eusebius, now of Nicomedia, thinks he runs the whole Church because he deserted his charge at Berytus and cast longing glances at the church in Nicomedia—and

nobody stopped him—and has put himself at the head of these apostates as well, daring even to send commendatory letters for them in all directions, trying to inveigle some of the ignorant, by whatever means, into this lowlife heresy that is hostile to Christ, I felt as if I had to speak up now.

Alexander went on to list the main followers of Arius: six priests (including Arius himself), six deacons, and two "who once were called bishops." He set out in detail what they asserted "in complete contradiction to the Scriptures, and wholly of their own devising." And he warned the bishops to "pay no attention to anything that Eusebius writes to you," because he had taken up their cause, even though nearly a hundred bishops of Egypt and Libya had come together and decided to anathematize Arius and all who accepted his shameless heresies.[9]

Meanwhile, Arius was corresponding with Eusebius. We have one of his letters addressed to "his very dear lord, the faithful man of God, orthodox Eusebius," in which he describes himself as "unjustly persecuted by Pope Alexander on account of that all-conquering truth which you also 'defend as with a shield'"—quoting the Greek version of Psalm 47:9. (The bishop of Alexandria had traditionally been called "pope" since very early times. It did not mean he had the same authority as the bishop of Rome. It was, in both cases, an honorific, fatherly title.)

Arius and his friends were suffering terribly, he told Eusebius. "I want to tell you that the bishop is on a rampage. He's persecuting us severely. He's in full sail against us. He's driven us out of the city as atheists because we don't agree with what he preaches in public."

And what was Alexander preaching? Arius summarizes: "God has always been, and the Son has always been. Father and Son exist together. The Son has his existence unbegotten along with God; he is always being begotten, without having been begotten. God does not precede the Son by thought or by any interval, however small. God has always been; the Son has always been; the Son is from God himself."[10]

Allowing for a little polemical exaggeration—Alexander almost certainly didn't say the Son was "unbegotten," which is probably Arius's notion of the logical consequence of what Alexander did say—what Arius says Alexander was preaching sounds very much like orthodox Catholic Christianity to modern ears. But Arius could never get over his simple time-bound notion of God. If the Son was begotten, that happened at a particular point in time, so there was a time before.

"But as for us," Arius continued, "what do we believe? And what have we taught, and what do we teach?"

Here Arius sets out his own creed: "That the Son is *not* unbegotten, nor in any way part of the unbegotten." Again, it seems that Arius believes that the only alternative to being begotten in time is not being begotten at all.

"We are persecuted because we say, 'The Son had a beginning, but God is without beginning.' This is really the cause of our persecution—and, likewise, because we say that he is from nothing. And we say this because he is neither part of God nor of any lower essence. For this we are persecuted. You know the rest."

Notice the distinction Arius makes: the Son . . . but God. The Son is *not* God, according to Arius. This is probably what was most shocking to Bishop Alexander, because Christians believe that the Son, the Word, *is* God. (See the beginning of the Gospel of John, for example.) And in some way Arius apparently believed it, too; in the same letter he says he teaches that the Son "subsisted before time, and before all ages as God," which seems pretty clear. But right after that Arius adds that "he was not, before he was begotten." Arius used the same kind of language when he wrote to Alexander, trying to explain himself: "created before times and before ages," and "begotten apart from time before all things."

Yet in spite of Arius's insistence that the begetting of the Son was "apart from time" or "before time," he still asserted vehemently that "there was a time when he was not." And in spite of his insistence that the Son subsisted as God, Arius continued to distinguish God from the Son: "God is before all things, being Monad and Beginning of all; for which reason he is also before the Son."[11]

Already, Arius's ideas were spreading, as Alexander grumpily noted. "There was a time when he was not" was a catchy slogan—in Greek it sounds like a line from a nursery rhyme. You can chant it easily in a street riot. And Arius had a great deal of help from Eusebius of Nicomedia. In fact, what became known as "Arianism" was really Eusebius's pet project. (The historian Lewis Ayres prefers to call the movement "Eusebianism,"[12] because the real movers of it were Eusebius of Nicomedia and, to a much lesser extent, the historian Eusebius of Caesarea. But it was always called Arianism by the writers we remember as the great theologians of the time.)

Why did the bishop of Nicomedia latch on to the ideas of an obscure priest way down in Alexandria? He might have thought Arius was right. He might well have been so thoroughly convinced by Arius's arguments that he felt bound in conscience to support Arius against his bishop.

But most writers on the other side attributed less noble motives to Eusebius. Ambition was the usual motive they cited. Leapfrogging over other candidates and the rules of the Church, Eusebius had made himself bishop of the imperial capital in the East. How better could he prove he was important in the Church than by giving himself authority over other bishops—like Alexander?

The modern writer Rod Bennett suggests a more benevolent reason for Eusebius's interference. In Arius's system of Christianity, Eusebius might have seen something much easier for pagans to accept, especially educated, philosophical pagans.[13] It didn't require them to believe that God, the perfect First Principle, had sullied himself by taking on imperfect and smelly human flesh. That idea was scandalous to philosophical pagans. But it was easy to swallow the idea that God had created a being far superior to humankind, but far below God himself, to bridge the gap between the divine and the material. Arianism gave the pagans a kind of Christianity Lite, easy to accept without changing ingrained habits of thought.

And Eusebius might have had very strong reasons for wanting to make Christianity more acceptable to recalcitrant pagans. Meanwhile, Licinius, the Eastern emperor, was getting increasingly impatient with the

Christians. The Christians needed to be careful. One wrong move could bring the Age of Persecution back.

Up Close and Personal:

WHO ATTENDED THE COUNCIL OF NICAEA?

Of the 1,800 bishops in the world at the time, only a small number could make the arduous trip to Nicaea for the council. Only five came from the churches in the western part of the Empire.

Athanasius of Alexandria—who was there as an adviser—said there were 318 bishops in attendance. Other ancients give other numbers, so historians debate the matter, with some saying no more than 250 bishops were there.

Some of the bishops had suffered during the recent persecution of Diocletian. They arrived maimed, and the Emperor Constantine greeted them by kissing their wounds. Many arrived with an entourage of secretaries, theologians, and servants, so the total number of attendees was probably well over a thousand.

A later legend, attested only in documents of the second millennium, claims that St. Nicholas of Myra (today known as Santa Claus) was there, and that he punched the heretic Arius in the nose, bringing forth a profusion of blood. Though St. Nicholas may indeed have attended (he appears on one ancient list), it's unlikely that such an act of violence would have gone unnoticed by early attendees and historians.

It's certainly a good tale. It's likely no more than that.

Unity and Division

Licinius and Constantine were finding it harder and harder to get along. Constantine had always been the obviously stronger member of the partnership, and Licinius seems to have resented that more as the years went by. And Licinius was getting more paranoid. Since Constantine favored the Christians and Licinius was still a pagan, Licinius imagined that the Christians must all be secret Constantine boosters, spies, saboteurs boring from within. He was convinced that they were praying for their hero Constantine to prevail over him—"such was the reckoning of an evil conscience," as the historian Eusebius comments.

The more he plotted against Constantine, the more Licinius mistreated the Christians. First he kicked them out of his palace. Then he insisted that officers in the city police forces make pagan sacrifices or lose their rank. He started to impose impossible regulations on the Christians. He separated the sexes, for example: only women could teach women, and women and men could not worship together—after all, Christians had been chopping at the root of Roman family values with their absurd doctrine that "there is neither male nor female" (see Galatians 3:28). Christian worship was allowed only outside, not in a church or house or any other building. That way he could keep an eye on the rabble. And bishops (whom he thought were all plotting against him) were prohibited from holding meetings or even communicating with one another.

Since Christians couldn't carry on their business without breaking the rules, they quickly began to get into trouble. But Licinius didn't always wait for them to get into trouble. He and his compliant governors sometimes arrested one of the bishops without even bothering to give a legally plausible reason. Some of those bishops were never seen again. Some were publicly and gruesomely executed, their bodies torn into little pieces and thrown into the sea as fish food. Churches were knocked down. And rumor had it that Licinius was planning more and worse: another universal persecution like the Great Persecution.

Once again, Christians began to flee to the wilderness. Refugee camps appeared in deserts, hills, and valleys.

But some tried to minimize the damage. Eusebius of Nicomedia tried his best to keep on Licinius's good side. The man was a peacemaker at heart, especially if he could advance his own interests while making peace. There were rumors that he made himself more useful to Licinius than he was publicly willing to admit—rumors that Eusebius had spies reporting on Constantine's movements, and much darker rumors that some of the martyred bishops had been reported to the authorities by Eusebius.

And then it was over. In 324, the long-simmering feud finally broke into open war. Constantine and Licinius met with huge armies, and Constantine won.

Eusebius had backed the wrong horse, if we believe the rumors. But the rest of the Christians rejoiced. Once more the Empire was united under one strong and competent emperor—and he was an open friend of the Christians. "Constantine, the most mighty victor, resplendent with every virtue godliness bestows—together with his son Crispus, an emperor most dear to God and in every way like his father—recovered the East that belonged to them, and made the Roman Empire into a single united whole as in days of old." Thus that other Eusebius, the famous historian, told the story of Constantine's victory, adding that the sky was blue and everyone broke into spontaneous song and dance.[14]

Now that the whole Empire was in the hands of Constantine, religious freedom was unambiguously the law of the land. It was the law even for pagans, Constantine reiterated. "Let those who still delight in error be made welcome to the same degree of peace and tranquility that those who believe have. For it may be that the restoration of equal privileges to all will prevail to lead them into the straight path. Let no one molest another, but let everyone do as his soul desires."[15]

Nevertheless, Constantine hoped his united Empire could also be united in faith eventually. "For I was aware that, if I should succeed in establishing a common harmony of feeling among all the servants of God, the general course of affairs would also experience a change corresponding to the pious desires of them all."

But instead, the whole East was in an uproar over some trivial question of words.

Constantine was a soldier, not a philosopher. He had no patience for an "unprofitable question" like this. He wrote to both Alexander and Arius saying that Arius ought never to have brought up the question—it "ought not to have been conceived at all; or, if it was conceived, it ought to have been buried in deep silence." And he hinted that he was more than a little impatient with Alexander for taking it seriously and bothering to call the other priests together to render an opinion on the subject. "It was wrong in the first place to propose such questions as these, or to reply to them when they were posed." Only a love of argument for its own sake could have induced people to worry about questions like this. "Let therefore both the unguarded question and the inconsiderate answer receive your mutual forgiveness."[16] Why can't we all just get along?

It was too late for such a simple reconciliation, in spite of Constantine's admonitions. Arius was too stubborn, and Alexander was convinced that the question actually was important. To his mind, Arius's doctrine led to a direct denial of the very heart of Christianity. If the Son was not God himself, then God didn't come to save his own people from their sin, and there was no real reconciliation between God and humankind. Alexander knew the truth instinctively, but he felt out of his league debating with Arius. Arius had all the tricks of logic and rhetoric up his sleeve, all the techniques that won applause at philosophical debates. What Alexander needed was an adviser, even a speechwriter, who could debate with Arius on the same professional level.

And luckily he had one right in his own office. Alexander's secretary was a young man of colossal talents, easily able to meet Arius on his own ground, and easily able to demolish his specious logic. The young man's name was Athanasius, and you might say that he saved the Christian faith.

A Gathering of the Whole Church

No one paid much attention to Constantine's recommendation. Or, rather, they paid it all the reverence due to a message from the most august emperor of the world, and then proceeded to ignore it. But Arius and his party were taking their message to the streets, threatening more riots in the very riot-prone city of Alexandria. And Alexander refused to back down from his insistence on what the Church had always taught. Constantine grew more and more annoyed.

Constantine genuinely cared about peace and unity. He was a soldier, but war was not the goal for him. It seems very clear that his ultimate goal was the peace and prosperity of the Empire, and he looked forward to a day when he could hang up his sword forever. And Christianity, the religion of the Prince of Peace, ought to be the unifying principle that allowed him to do it. His natural instinct was to tell people that everything would be all right if they could just be nice to each other. He had tried to sort out the Donatist schism in Africa, and eventually had given up on that; he wasn't willing to persecute even people as stubborn as the Donatists. So when they refused to give up property that all the other bishops and secular judges and Constantine himself had determined belonged to the Catholic Church, Constantine just gave up and let them keep it, compensating the Church from his own pocket.

But now this Arian controversy was even more of a headache. What could be done about it?

A Spanish bishop named Ossius (sometimes rendered Hosius) was Constantine's most trusted religious adviser, and he had a brilliant idea. Call together the bishops of the whole Church. The Empire was united and at peace; travel was safe and easy. It would take some organizing, but it could be done. Get the bishops together, have them make a decision, and the whole Church would have to fall in line.

Constantine jumped on this suggestion. It was so simple! Immediately he set about putting it into action. Just a day away from Nicomedia was a port called Nicaea, easily accessible from anywhere. He sent out his summons to all the bishops, paying their travel expenses and putting the Roman government transit system (which was thorough and well-developed) at their disposal.

Ultimately 318 bishops showed up—the largest gathering of bishops in the history of the Church so far, and the only one that included bishops from the whole Church since the Council of Jerusalem, when the original apostles met to discuss the Gentile question (see Acts 15). The pope—that is, the bishop of Rome—couldn't make it, but he sent two priests to represent him. It was a grand spectacle to see so many bishops at once, and the general public filled the spectators' areas to listen to some of the preliminary debates. Even pagan philosophers joined the fun—some out of genuine curiosity, others to make fun of the Christians.[17] People from town came just to see the parade of bishops of all nations. Even Scythia, exotic land of barbarian cowboys, and Persia, traditional enemy of Rome for generations, were represented.

Every once in a while, one of the spectators might point to a bishop carried in on a litter, a man whose mangled body bore witness to the tortures of Licinius or the Great Persecution before him. The honor paid to these living martyrs was an impressive reminder of how far the Church had come in a very short time.

And of course everyone wanted a glimpse of the two men who had started the whole uproar, Arius and Alexander. Alexander, a frail old man who needed help to get around, was a bit of a disappointment, although his young archdeacon and assistant Athanasius looked like a man to watch. But Arius was a rock star. He was tall, a good speaker, and a very thoughtful-looking man. Fangirls followed him wherever he went. He must have something to say.[18]

The Western bishops and representatives probably found all this hubbub baffling, and maybe a little appalling. They had heard that Greeks loved an argument, but until they saw it with their own eyes they didn't know how true it was. Arius's ideas hadn't made any real progress in the West; most Westerners had heard of them only as those odd propositions that had the East in turmoil. Now the Westerners were plunged into the middle of polite debates or shouting matches about ideas they could barely understand. Making it worse, by this time most Westerners probably knew very little Greek, so all this rapid-fire philosophizing was impossible for them to follow.

When the main session of the Council of Nicaea finally opened, the public circus was left outside. The emperor himself gave the keynote speech—in Latin, which must have been a relief to the Westerners. An interpreter translated for the Greek-speaking majority in the audience.

Constantine thanked the bishops for making such an arduous journey and told them how much he had longed to see the spectacle of so many of them gathered in one place. It was terrible, he said, that just as they had finally gained peace from their enemies, Christians should be fighting each other. The scriptures teach us all we need to know about the nature of God, he noted. Let's look into them, find the answers to our questions, and stop all this bickering over words.

Everyone agreed that the emperor had spoken well. Of course he had spoken well: he was the emperor. But some present might have privately wondered who appointed Constantine bishop.

Arius was given the chance to speak next—and that may have doomed him. He expressed his ideas confidently, and so clearly and distinctly that no one could misunderstand what he believed. Most of the bishops were stunned. They might not be able to articulate exactly what was wrong, but they knew wrong when they heard it, and this was wrong.

Alexander and Eusebius of Nicomedia then joined the debate. But the surprise star was Athanasius. Alexander turned over most of his debating duties to the young archdeacon, who demolished Arius's and Eusebius's arguments with ease. Arius had walked in a rock star, but the rock star who walked out would be Athanasius. And neither Arius nor Eusebius would ever forgive him for it.

There was much debate still to be had, but eventually it was suggested that the council should come up with some sort of statement of belief that would mark the boundaries of true Christian teaching. There were many schools of thought represented at Nicaea, but the point wasn't to establish one narrow straitjacket of orthodox thinking into which everyone had to fit. The point was to mark the large space within which one could reason and speculate as much as one liked, but outside which the thought could no longer be called Christian.

Eusebius of Nicomedia brought out his own statement of belief, and it seems he badly miscalculated the mood of the other bishops. Until now they had treated him with respect, but when his statement was read to the assembly, it caused such an outburst that the whole business of the council stopped. It couldn't start again until Eusebius's statement was very theatrically torn to bits while the other bishops watched.

Now that other Eusebius, the historian, stepped up. He suggested that the baptismal creed used in Palestine was something everyone could agree on. And everyone could agree on it. That was precisely why the majority found it inadequate. After Eusebius of Nicomedia's statement, they wanted to make sure that no one could think himself an orthodox Catholic Christian if he held to the doctrines of Arius.

So the creed they ultimately came up with was one the Arians could not agree to at all, because it insisted that the Son was of the same being or substance as the Father. The word in Greek that expressed that idea was *homoousios*—which we usually translate as "consubstantial" or "of the same being."

At first, many of the bishops weren't sure about that word. You can't find it in the scriptures. But ultimately they were convinced that it was the only way to exclude Arianism. And so at last, by a huge majority, the council voted to accept the Nicene Creed:

> We believe in one God, the Father almighty, maker of all things visible and invisible.
>
> And in one Lord Jesus Christ, the Son of God, the only-begotten of the Father; God from God and Light from Light; true God from true God; begotten, not made; consubstantial with the Father; by whom all things were made, both in heaven and on earth; who for the sake of us men and for our salvation descended, became incarnate, and was made man; suffered,

arose again the third day, and ascended into the heavens, and
will come again to judge the living and the dead.

Also in the Holy Spirit.

But the holy Catholic and apostolic Church anathematizes
those who say there was a time when he was not, and he was
not before he was begotten, and he was made from that which
did not exist, and those who assert that he is of other substance
or essence than the Father, or that he was created, or is susceptible of change.[19]

Those anathemas at the end struck at the heart of Arian teaching, and
there was no way an Arian could support them. So it's a little surprising
to see that Eusebius of Caesarea agreed to this creed. Somehow he con-
torted his thought to suppose that, although he had been sympathetic to
Arius and the other Eusebius, there was nothing in it he couldn't agree
to. "As to the anathemas published by them at the end of the creed," he
wrote to his diocese back home, "we thought it without offense because
they forbade the use of words not in Scripture, from which almost all the
confusion and disorder in the Church have come."[20] In other words, we
can still have the opinions if we just don't use the words for them.

This was a preview of things to come.[21]

Constantine declared himself very pleased with the work of the council. They had sorted everything out, and now we could all get back to living
in peace and harmony. He was pleased with his own part in the affair, too:
"I myself, who, as one of you, rejoice exceedingly in being your fellow-ser-
vant, undertook the investigation of the truth." The emperor had thoroughly enjoyed playing bishop. He would have to do it again someday.[22]

As for Arius, who had started the whole uproar, he was sent into exile.
And soon after, Eusebius of Nicomedia was sent out with Constantine's
footprint on his rear. Not only had he been the one who taught Arianism
to the rest of the world, but he was a "participant in the tyrant's savagery."
The stories of Eusebius supporting Licinius had reached Constantine's
ears. "I won't say anything right now about his outrageous actions against
me personally," Constantine wrote to the church in Nicomedia after he

dismissed Eusebius. Then he went on to describe those outrageous actions in detail. "At the moment when the opposing armies were about to clash, he sent spies to report on me. He almost gave the tyrant armed assistance. Don't think I'm not prepared to prove it."[23]

Orthodoxy was restored; Arius and Eusebius of Nicomedia were in exile; and the emperor was firmly on the side of the traditional doctrine of the Catholic Church. It looked as though everything was right in the best of all possible empires.

But the Arians weren't finished yet.

YOU BE THE JUDGE:

Did Constantine create the Bible?

The Emperor Constantine is like the Elvis of the ancient world, the subject of many urban legends. It's easy to see why. His stature was gigantic. He ruled much of the world as sole emperor. His genuine accomplishments were colossal and revolutionary: he proposed new notions of public morality; he invented religious freedom and brought about the end of Christian persecution; he funded a new wave of monumental public works; he established a new capital, named it for himself, and made it a major metropolis.

Constantine was a singular figure. He played a pivotal role in history. He exercised great power. To many casual observers, it seems natural to credit him with more than he actually did.

Some, for example, said he created the Bible as we know it— excluding books that Christians had formerly considered authoritative: the Gospel of Thomas, for example, the Gospel of Judas, the Acts of Paul, and others that are now known as apocryphal.

But the truth is that the canon was well settled long before Constantine was born. The Muratorian Canon, probably produced in the mid-100s, is a list almost identical to the table of contents in a modern New Testament. Long before then, the four gospels were accepted together as a canonical unit. By the end of that century, St. Irenaeus cited twenty-one of the twenty-seven books in passing—and he cites none of the apocrypha as authorities.

So where did the myth of Constantine's canon come from?

In the year 331, Constantine commissioned the production of fifty Bibles to be sent to the major churches throughout the world. We don't know for sure what was in those Bibles—perhaps only the four gospels, or only the New Testament. It wasn't a big news story at the time; nor did it stir controversy at all. Whatever was in those books was seen as conventional. It corresponded to the tradition received from the early Church, confirmed in the works of the earlier Church Fathers.

Sometimes, too, Constantine is "blamed" for ritualizing the Church—imposing a liturgy on a previously informal Church. But again, the documents of the fourth century show no rupture with the Church of the third and second centuries. From the first century forward, the Church celebrated the sacraments— Baptism, Eucharist, Penance—according to forms established since the time of the apostles.

Constantine was a generous patron of the Church. He was not a creative thinker in matters of religion.

Chapter 4

The Empire Christianized

In the year 325, Constantine had been delighted to act the part of a bishop at the Council of Nicaea. In 326, he killed his son and his wife.

Crispus, "an emperor most dear to God and in every way like his father" (as Eusebius the historian described him just two years earlier), was executed for treason. And then, shortly afterward, Constantine's wife, Fausta, was smothered in the bath.

What happened? As anyone who knows politics might guess, the stories were many and varied, some of them involving dark rumors of a love affair between the illegitimate Crispus and the emperor's wife. But the most likely and most often repeated story was that Fausta, jealous of Crispus's success (which left her own legitimate sons in the shadows), accused him of treason. Constantine believed her and didn't wait to sort out the facts. When, after he had killed his own son, he discovered that the accusations were false, he was naturally furious and beside himself with guilt; Fausta was executed—or murdered—as punishment for inducing Constantine to murder his son.

It was a tragedy that Shakespeare could have written. And it set a kind of pattern for Constantine's family. The lesson Constantine's young sons—Constantius, Constantine, and Constans (the emperor had definite tastes in names)—learned from it was that there are few problems that can't be solved by murdering a relative.

And one more thing the tragedy showed—again, if the usual story is true—was that it was easy to impose on Constantine. He was broadly honest and vigorously active, and he really seems to have had the best interests

of the Empire at heart. But he was gullible. And there were people willing
to take advantage of that quality.

The Arians Are Back

Nicaea had forced the Catholic Church to look deeply into the nature of
God. We might almost call the Arian turmoil providential. (A century
later, Augustine of Hippo would say as much.) It was the Arian question
that forced many Christians, who had always believed that Jesus Christ,
the Son of God, was himself God, to look into the implications of that
belief and articulate exactly what it meant.

That should have been enough. The bishops of the whole Church had
met and decided by an overwhelming majority that the opinions of Arius
were contrary to what Christians had always believed. And they had come
up with a statement of faith to define exactly what Christians did believe
about the divinity of the Son.

But the Arians didn't take their defeat lying down. They got to work.
They couldn't get around the Council of Nicaea; it had really happened.
So they had to find a way to accept the fact of Nicaea while still holding
on to their Arian opinions.

Arius took one route. He confessed an almost, but not quite, Nicene
faith in a letter to the emperor. He left out the word *homoousios*, which
the council had insisted on as proof against Arianism—but, on the other
hand, he said nothing about a time when the Son was not, or about how
the Father was more glorious than the Son by an infinity of glories, or any
of the other things that had come to be known as distinctively Arian. He
wrote: "And so we beseech your Piety, Emperor most beloved of God, that
we who are ordained to the ministry, and hold the faith and sentiments of
the Church and of the holy Scriptures, may by your pacific and devoted
Piety be reunited to our mother, the Church, all superfluous questions
and the wranglings arising from them being avoided."[1]

There it was: Arius's master stroke. Constantine was well known for
his impatience with "unprofitable questions." If Arius could convince him

that he had accepted the Nicene faith in its broad outlines, then anyone who quibbled was now the enemy of peace, not Arius. After all, Arius was willing to be reasonable, wasn't he?

It worked. Constantine revoked Arius's exile and sent a letter to Alexander directing the old bishop to take him back in the diocese of Alexandria.

But it was a bit late for that. In 327, Alexander died. He may never have read Constantine's letter. If he did, he was too ill to either protest or to accede.

Meanwhile, Eusebius of Nicomedia took a more direct approach. He simply accepted the term *homoousios* and stated that now he completely agreed with everything Nicaea had concluded. "We declare that we entirely concur with you in the faith—and also that, having closely considered the meaning of the term *homoousios*, we have been wholly studious of peace, having never followed the heresy."[2]

Once again this letter, addressed to some bishop or other Church official who was asked to petition Constantine on Eusebius's behalf, went right for Constantine's soft point. All Eusebius wanted was peace, he claimed. We might be forgiven for raising our eyebrows when we come to that part where he says he has "never followed the heresy," although perhaps in a quibbling sense it's true: are you really following the heresy when you lead it?

At any rate, Eusebius saw no reason why he shouldn't be taken back into the fold now that he had satisfied everyone that he agreed with Nicaea 100 percent, "especially since it has seemed good to your Piety to deal tenderly with and recall even him who was primarily accused"—by which he meant Arius. Since Eusebius certified himself thoroughly orthodox, anyone who stood in the way of readmitting him to the Church must be the enemy of peace. And what the emperor wanted most of all was peace.

Once again, it worked. Soon after Arius returned, Eusebius of Nicomedia was reinstated as well.

Constantine was not being unreasonable in taking the two heretics back once they had confessed their faith in what looked like a Nicene form. In fact, he was showing one of the best aspects of his character. He was impulsive and hot-tempered—with disastrous results for his son Crispus—but he forgave like a Christian.

Still, he was gullible. Arius and Eusebius had not changed their opinions at all. They had just decided to bide their time, publicly accepting the Nicene Creed while privately holding on to the same beliefs they had held before.

At any rate, Constantine was certainly bored with the whole dispute by now. He had enjoyed playing bishop, but it was time to move on to bigger things. And Constantine had one of the biggest plans ever hatched in the mind of a Roman emperor.

Up Close and Personal:
ST. ATHANASIUS OF ALEXANDRIA

"The world," said St. Jerome, "awoke to find itself Arian." He was marveling at the suddenness with which the Arian heresy overtook the Church. The Arian emperor mocked Athanasius's seemingly futile struggle for orthodoxy, summing it up as "Athanasius against the world." Some historians believe that, at the heresy's peak, it claimed the allegiance of 80 percent of the world's bishops.

Athanasius held his ground. At the Council of Nicaea, he had served as secretary to Alexander, the bishop who was first confronted by Arius. A few years later, as Alexander lay dying, he himself appointed Athanasius as his successor.

He would serve as bishop of Alexandria for forty-five years, though he spent many of those years in exile. He was opposed by officials of Church and state. He was pursued by assassins and stood trial for murder. (Athanasius was exonerated when he produced the supposed "victim," still alive.) Once, he was fleeing down the Nile River, and a military boat drew near. The soldiers told him they were looking for Athanasius; he informed them that Athanasius was "not far away" and urged them to hurry onward. They did.

He traveled to Byzantium to appeal to the emperor, and to Rome to consult with the pope. He lived for a while in his family's tomb. Through all this, he wrote constantly—sophisticated theological treatises as well as pleading letters. He produced the first defense of the Holy Spirit's divinity. He even published a best-selling biography of the monk St. Anthony. He ended his days at home in Alexandria. He is remembered as one of the "Great" Fathers of the Church and is counted as a Doctor of the Church.

A New Rome

Constantine was emperor of the whole Roman Empire now, and it was obvious to him that things had changed since the days of Augustus three centuries before. Rome had conquered the world, but Rome herself was increasingly irrelevant to the rest of the Empire. It was still the biggest city in the West, but most of the action now was in the East. The West was declining; the East was recovering from the plagues and prospering. Most of the big cities and the larger part of the population were in the East.

Previous emperors had already acknowledged in practice that the city of Rome didn't make a very useful capital anymore. Remember that Constantine and Licinius had issued their famous edict of toleration in Milan, which had become the effective capital of the West. Rome was too far from the hot spots where emperors had to do their business.

The Roman Empire had two big problem points, which together required the attention of most of its defensive forces. One was the border with Persia (or Parthia, depending on the era) in the East. The two great empires had been almost continuously at war for generations. Sometimes there was a fragile peace, but one side or the other was always tempted to make a surprise raid across the border, and then it was back to war again.

The other difficult frontier was the River Danube, which formed the border with Germany. We would call it Germany, at any rate, but at the time, its inhabitants were tribes of uncivilized warriors whose main business was raiding. Sometimes they raided each other, and that was fine. But often they poured across the border into Gaul and ran off with loot and women. It was necessary to keep a large part of the Roman military nearby to discourage these proto-Germans.

Rome was far from either of those two problem frontiers. But there was a little town that seemed to be just about perfectly placed. It was near enough to both problem areas for the emperor to get to either one fairly quickly. But it was also one of the most naturally defensible towns in the Empire, surrounded on three sides by water, leaving the one land side easily defended by walls and a relatively small force. The name of the place was Byzantium. And Constantine's grand plan was to take that little town and turn it into a magnificent new Rome, the new capital of the Roman Empire.

Certainly, strategic considerations went into his decision. But it was also true that the old Rome was a difficult city for the Christian emperor. In spite of a large Christian population, Rome was still very pagan. Its Senate was full of crusty obstructionists who were suspicious of the new Christian order. Constantine let them have their way, but he had to be uncomfortable with the entrenched paganism of the Roman establishment. A new capital, built to his specifications, could be Christian from the start. Constantine would have no trouble getting along with the establishment there, because he would get to decide who the establishment was. And instead of pagan temples on every corner, he could fill the place with magnificent Christian churches.

What to call it, though? Constantine's usual taste in names made the obvious suggestion: Constantinople.

In 328, the new capital was officially founded. Right on the border between East and West, between Europe and Asia, a new and spectacular city began to rise from the old town of Byzantium. The old guard in Rome must have snickered at first; Constantine thought he could just decree a city, when it had taken Rome a thousand years to get where it was today. But as the glorious new capital took shape, the news must have filtered back to Rome: Constantine is actually doing it. He's making this New Rome into a real city. And it's a Christian city.

The New Order

The new capital was a visible manifestation of the new order. Constantine still insisted on tolerance for all religions, but he was going to make it clear which one he favored: "Let them have their temples of falsehood if they like; we have the glorious edifice of God's truth."[3]

The whole Empire was taking on a more Christian tone. It didn't happen overnight, but the trend was obvious. Constantine was building churches all over the place. Christian clergy were partners in government, as the pagan priests had been before them. Legislation favored Christian morality: crucifixion was ended as a means of execution; beast shows—where criminals (in the past including Christians) were thrown to wild animals for the entertainment of the spectators in the arena—were outlawed; slave owners were actually punished for murdering their slaves; and the emperor promised aid to parents who would otherwise have to sell their children into slavery.

Under the smile of the emperor, Christian institutions flourished. Structures built to help the helpless during the famine and plagues were expanded. The wealthy, who had donated showy public works in pagan times, now found it prestigious to have their names associated with institutions to help the poor and sick. Monasteries popped up like mushrooms; a more organized form of the monastic community, the innovation of a former military man named Pachomius, began to spread throughout the East—the direct ancestor of the great monasteries that kept the flame of civilization burning through the "Dark Ages" to come. And those monasteries themselves became centers of Christian charity, as the monks sought some way of living the Gospel demand that we take care of the least of Christ's brethren.

The new pop-culture heroes were no longer demigods such as Hercules or Perseus; they were the martyrs—men, women, and children who had chosen to die rather than abandon Christ. Their graves were popular pilgrimage sites. Churches were built over their relics. It was safe to be a Christian now, but the memory of the persecutions was still fresh.

Of course, there were still many pagans, and occasionally an anti-Christian mob attacked some Christians, or a Christian mob attacked some pagans. With Christianity now the dominant religion, it was inevitable that some Christians wouldn't act much like Christians.

But although pagans were still numerous enough to form mobs, it must have been clear to all but the most nostalgic that there wasn't much life left in paganism. The few pagan writers of any note in those days were writing mostly starchy imitations of the great writings of the past. It was among the Christians that the great minds of the age could be found.

The same was true in art. Christians had adapted pagan traditions to their needs, but now Christianity began to develop its own artistic tradition—one that continues today in the iconography of the Eastern churches and in the statuary of the West.

Probably Christianity's greatest accomplishment was general recognition of the simple idea that all human beings are valuable, and the concrete deeds that idea inspired. No one had cared about the poor before the Christians came along. Now the emperor himself shed a tear for them and promised to help when they were in extreme circumstances.

We should remember Christianity's accomplishments in all the ugly wrangling that followed.

Showdown: Athanasius vs. Arius, Part II

In 328, after frail old Alexander passed away, Athanasius was made bishop of Alexandria. He was just a little over thirty years old—very young for a bishop. And the choice was not made without loud disagreements. Alexandria was the sort of city where a riot could break out over anything, and the position of bishop was probably the most coveted office in the city, now that bishops were entrusted with much of the ordinary business of government.

Constantine wrote Athanasius a letter demanding that he accept the supposedly reformed Arians back into communion. "Now that you know what my will is, grant free admission to all who wish to enter the Church. For if I learn that you have hindered any who claim membership, or kept them from entering, I will immediately send someone to depose you at my command and remove you from your place."[4]

This letter put Athanasius in a difficult position. If he refused to allow Arius and the others back into communion in Alexandria, he was now the enemy of unity in the emperor's eyes. But if he did reinstate the Arians, they could claim to represent the real Catholic Church, as they had done before. And Athanasius was perfectly aware that they hadn't really changed their opinions. All you had to do was listen on the street in Alexandria; that little chant "There was a time when he was not" could still be heard everywhere.

What Athanasius recognized—and he was proved right by later events—was that the Arians had a master plan. The strategy went something like this:

1. They would claim to accept Nicaea, insisting, against all logic, that their beliefs were consistent with the Nicene Creed.
2. They would wangle important positions for Arian bishops—if necessary by ejecting the current bishop by whatever means came to hand.
3. They would portray the orthodox Nicene side as stubborn and inimical to peace, thus rousing the emperor against them.

The new Arian strategy had its first big test in Antioch, the great capital of Syria, famous as the place where the name "Christian" was first used (see Acts 11:26). Eustathius, bishop of Antioch, had been one of the pillars of orthodoxy at the Council of Nicaea. Now he entered into a war of pamphlets with Eusebius of Caesarea, who accused him of Sabellianism—a heresy that denies that the Son of God is in any way distinct from the Father. The historian Theodoret says that the whole thing was engineered by Eusebius of Nicomedia. Whatever the real start of it was, Eustathius was deposed, and an Arian sympathizer took his place. But a large number of the Christians of Antioch refused to recognize the replacement, prompting a schism in that city that would last for decades. Nevertheless, the Arian sympathizer was the bishop officially recognized by the imperial government. The Arians had won in one of the greatest cities of the Empire.

Athanasius saw what was going on very clearly. He saw, for example, that the Arians were making a deal with the Melitian schismatics in Alexandria, which gave them more of a base of support than they'd had before. And it's possible that Athanasius reacted a bit too vigorously to this news.

What actually happened is hard to sort out, because the later accusations against Athanasius were so bizarrely overblown that we can hardly tell where the truth ends and the wild rumors begin. We know that there were riots between the Melitians and the Catholic party of Athanasius. Mobs of Athanasius's supporters kept Melitians from entering the churches (and remember how Constantine had specifically warned against this type of behavior). Mobs and countermobs clashed in the streets. And it seems as though Athanasius had some of the Melitians arrested by the civil authorities. Under Constantine's new world order, the bishop had a lot of power, and no one quite knew yet exactly how much power. Where the emperor had made rules that had to do with the Church, it made sense to see the bishop as the executive power in his diocese.

So how much of the violence happened with Athanasius's approval, or at least his winking acquiescence? We don't know. We do know that Athanasius was panicking a little. Here it was only five years after the Council of Nicaea, and it seemed as though the council's work was being undone. The Arians were back, and it looked as if they had the ear of the emperor.

Arius certainly saw the same trend. He decided to make a personal appeal to the emperor, pointing out that he had a lot of support for his faction.

That was a huge mistake.

Constantine hated factions, and Arius seemed to be saying that he had a large one that was ready to make trouble. The emperor responded with an angry letter and an order that Arius's works should be burned.

By this time, though, Arius really did have quite a following. Eusebius of Nicomedia, who claimed to be in complete agreement with the Nicene Creed, was back in good repute, and he was a clever puller of strings. He and his allies recognized that their real enemy was Athanasius. Constantine had no interest in abstract theology; all he wanted was peace in the Church. Make it obvious that Athanasius is the enemy of peace, and you've won the battle.

So accusations against Athanasius began to pour in—some involving heinous crimes. Among other things, he was accused of murdering a man and dismembering him to use his arm in some fiendish magical rite. People in the Mediterranean world of the 300s had a strong superstitious horror of magic, so the accusation, unlikely though it sounds to us, was not so implausible then.

Constantine decided to call a council at Tyre in Phoenicia to examine the charges, and demanded that Athanasius appear. When Athanasius got there, he realized that the deck was already stacked against him. He was able to refute the charge of murder and magic by producing the supposed victim, still alive and walking and using both arms. But a commission was sent to Egypt to investigate the other claims, and Athanasius couldn't help noticing that it was packed with Arians.

The commission came back and reported. There was enough evidence, they said, to condemn Athanasius. The council—also packed with Arians—voted to depose him.

Athanasius made one last desperate attempt to clear his name. He went straight to Constantine to plead his case. And he seemed to make some headway.

The Arian faction couldn't let that happen. They put forth one more accusation: that Athanasius was interfering with grain shipments from Egypt.

That was the most serious claim of all, because Egypt was the bread-basket of the East. Without Egyptian grain, the rest of the eastern Mediterranean would starve.

Did Constantine believe the claim? We don't know for certain. One story is that he did. The other story is that the accusation made him realize that Athanasius had powerful enemies who would stop at nothing.

Whatever his motivation, Constantine sent Athanasius off to exile in faraway Trier in Gaul, an area governed by his son Constantine II. Either he was getting rid of a troublemaker, or he was putting Athanasius at a safe distance from his enemies.

This was Athanasius's first exile.

Meanwhile, just as Athanasius was headed west, Arius died. He died almost unnoticed, because the whole fight wasn't about him anymore. His ideas had long since been taken over by more powerful forces using them as a way to consolidate power.

Just a year later, in 337, Constantine fell ill. At last, he decided, the end was near, and it was time to be baptized.

In those days it was very common for Christians to put off baptism until they were near death. The reasoning went this way: baptism washes away past sins, and I still have a lot of sins to get through before I die. The Church had no completely firm policy yet on how much repentance was allowed after baptism, but most Christians had the impression that a mortal sin committed after baptism was hard to get over.

So Constantine was baptized on his deathbed—by Eusebius of Nicomedia.

From that moment, the emperor refused to put on the imperial purple again. He died in his baptismal white.

Eastern Christians count Constantine as a saint. He was, after all, the man who built Constantinople. Westerners have never eagerly taken up the cult. But, whatever you think of his saintliness, it's only fair to say that Constantine was a sincere Christian who also sincerely loved the Roman Empire. After decades of instability and civil war, he brought peace and a return to prosperity. He tried to start the process of making the secular world work on Christian principles. He really did earn his common title, Constantine the Great.

Although it's a pity about his sons.

YOU BE THE JUDGE:

Weren't bishops originally elected by the people?

In the fourth century, local churches kept their own peculiar customs for choosing bishops. The crowd in Milan, on the verge of rioting, acclaimed Ambrose their bishop—when he had not yet been baptized. Their choice was confirmed by the emperor Gratian, and that was that.

John Chrysostom, a priest in Antioch, was chosen by the emperor Theodosius to lead the church in the capital city of Constantinople. He was so popular in his native Antioch that he had to be secreted away, after nightfall, by a military escort.

In Rome, the pope was selected by the priests of the city, and they almost always chose one of the deacons as the successor of Peter.

Being bishop was a hard job, and it involved a lot of politics and worldly unpleasantness. Gregory Nazianzen was tricked and pressured by his friend Basil into accepting the leadership of a small diocese. He never quite adapted to the promotion and wished he could go back to living in seclusion. Eventually he did—and he never quite forgave Basil.

Many candidates mightily resisted the appointment. Some went to extremes. Ephrem was a prodigiously effective deacon. He wrote hymns and directed choirs. He established a hospital and tended the sick. He heard a rumor, however, that he was about to be kicked up the ladder. So what did he do? He soiled his clothes and walked around the crowded parts of the city, drooling and talking to himself. Word got out that Ephrem had lost his mind, and another man was chosen as bishop. As soon as Ephrem heard, he bathed and put on new clothes and got back to work.

Chapter 5

Pope Constantius

Constantine left three sons and a number of other relatives. We don't know exactly what he intended to happen to the Empire after he died, but what did happen was that it was divided between the three sons.

An appalling massacre ensued, and almost everyone agrees that the perpetrator, or instigator, was Constantius, the son who became emperor of the East after his father's death. Constantius methodically eliminated nearly everyone who was a potential threat to his power—all the cousins and uncles who could have made some claim of their own to the imperial purple.

Other than Constantius's brothers, only two heirs were left: one sickly boy named Gallus, and his five-year-old brother, Julian. Even they might have been killed, but it seems that Eusebius of Nicomedia gave them some protection. The man may have been a schemer, but he was not a fiend.

That little boy Julian never forgot what his cousin Constantius had done. "Our fathers were brothers, sons of the same father," he wrote years later. "And close relations as we were, see how this most humane emperor treated us! He put to death six of our cousins, my father (who was his uncle), another of our uncles on my father's side, and my eldest brother—all without trial."[1]

The New Christian Landscape

Meanwhile, in the West, Constantine II ruled as emperor, controlling Gaul, Britain, and Spain. Constantine II was a big fan of Athanasius. And one of the new emperor's first acts was to send Athanasius back to Alexandria.

If we're to believe Constantine II, it was his late father's idea. He tells us that Athanasius had been sent west for his own protection. The only difficulty is that we're not sure if he was telling the truth or if he just wanted to be a thorn in his brother Constantius's side.

"I don't suppose it can have escaped your devout minds," he wrote to the church in Alexandria, "that Athanasius, the expositor of the venerated law, was sent in the nick of time to Gaul. Otherwise he might have suffered some irreparable injury from the perverseness of wicked men, since the ferocity of his bloodthirsty adversaries continually endangered his sacred life."[2]

Therefore, Constantine II continued, Athanasius had been sent away for his own protection. But the danger was over, and the elder Constantine had always intended to call Athanasius back when the time was right. He died before he could do that, the younger Constantine wrote, but "I have thought it proper to carry his wishes into effect, having inherited the task from our emperor of divine memory."[3]

Athanasius came back to a festive welcome in Alexandria. He wasn't universally beloved—he still had his enemies—but it was obvious where the great majority of the Christians stood.

And how did Constantius take the news that his interfering brother had sent Athanasius home? We can take a wild guess from the fact that, at just about the same time Athanasius was returning in triumph, Constantius was installing his new bishop of Constantinople: Eusebius of Nicomedia.

Yes, once again, the wily and ambitious Eusebius had managed to advance himself. Aside from Rome, Constantinople was now arguably the most prestigious see in the Church, since its bishop was the emperor Constantius's parish priest. In the East, the bishop of Constantinople was the only one who had as much influence as the bishop of Alexandria, and possibly more. So, in spite of canon law that still forbade bishops from jumping ship to take another diocese, Eusebius placed himself at the heart of the Empire.

And there was no question about how he was going to use this new power. Immediately, he made it obvious that he had Athanasius in his sights. He loudly insisted that the return of Athanasius was illegal. Constantius was emperor of the East, not Constantine II. Only Constantius could revoke Athanasius's exile, Eusebius said.

The predictable result was more riots in Alexandria. The Arians, encouraged by Constantius's obvious sympathy, formed mobs, which immediately ran into anti-Arian, pro-Nicene mobs.[4]

It got worse. From Alexandria, the riots and arguments spread throughout the East. "Everyone who asked what the fuss was about found something to argue about," wrote the historian Socrates. "As soon as he asked, he was already determined to get into the fight. All order was turned upside down by this general altercation."[5]

The whole East was arguing theology now. "But this agitation was confined to the East," Socrates continued. "The western parts of the Empire were perfectly peaceful, because they weren't willing to go against the decisions of the Council of Nicaea."[6]

Actually, Socrates was almost certainly exaggerating. It's true that there were mobs of Arians and anti-Arians, and they made a lot of noise and caused a lot of unrest. But most Christians probably looked on baffled. Faced with the two seeming extremes of Arianism on the one side and Athanasian orthodoxy on the other, some of them probably decided that the truth must lie somewhere in the middle.

It was Christianity's way of life that was attractive, not the theology. The theology was a necessary intellectual underpinning for the way of life, but most Christians followed Christ like little children. They accepted the theology they were taught in church, without pretending to understand it all. They knew that Christ was God, and they knew that Christ demanded that we love our neighbors and take care of the poor and helpless. If those in need were Arian Christians, they were still Christians.

So even while the theologians were wrangling, Christian institutions flourished.

The Least of These My Brethren

It's even possible that all the theological bickering advanced the cause of Christian charity. The historian of medicine Timothy S. Miller suggests that institutions of Christian charity in the cities actually increased in number because of the Arian controversy. With each side trying to out-Christian the other to prove that it was really following in the footsteps of Christ, poorhouses, hospitals, orphanages, and hostels sprang up in every city of any size.[7]

It's an encouraging theory. It suggests that there could have been a providential purpose for the increasingly ugly Arian dispute. Perhaps it was God's way of spurring Christians to action through vigorous competition.

But the truth may be simpler than that. These were all Christians, trying to do what Christ asked of them. They disagreed on theology, but they agreed on the duty of a Christian. "As you did it to one of the least of these my brethren, you did it to me," Christ said (see Matthew 25:40, 45).

In fact, both sides seem to have accused each other of not being Christlike enough. It is true that some of the most dedicated and selfless helpers of the poor were on the orthodox side—the desert monks of Egypt, for example, who had taught Athanasius and never wavered from orthodox belief. But it's also true that there were Arian sympathizers who founded charities in Eastern cities. The Arian dispute dominates Christian histories of the period because it's what most of the theological writers of the time wrote about. But real works of charity were going on almost unnoticed by history. The poor were being fed. The sick were being treated. Orphans found homes. Even the pagans had to admit that these things hadn't happened before the Christians came along.

The dispute continued to cause an uproar at least in theological circles. In 339, just two years after his triumphant return, Athanasius was exiled again. But meanwhile, Christians were doing the work of Christ. They were reaching out to people who had never had friends before in the Roman Empire. And that included the barbarian tribes outside the borders.

For example, in the year 340, a bishop named Ulfilas brought the Gospel to the Goths. It was more of an accomplishment than just preaching. Before he could give the Goths the scriptures, he had to invent literacy for them. The Goths were warriors; they had never seen the use of writing, so their language had never been written down. Ulfilas had to create an alphabet for them, based on the Greek alphabet, before he could begin to translate the Bible and the liturgy into Gothic.

It was a monumental work. Single-handed, Ulfilas translated the whole Bible into the Gothic language—"except for the books of Kings" (that is, the books we call 1 and 2 Samuel and 1 and 2 Kings), "which he omitted, because they are a mere narrative of military exploits. And the Gothic tribes were especially fond of war, and were in more need of restraints to check their military passions than of spurs to urge them on to deeds of war."[8]

History usually remembers Ulfilas as an Arian, and the Gothic tribes were in communion with the Arian branch of Christianity for a long time after him. But it may be fairer to say that Ulfilas was a Christian who had Constantine's impatience with unprofitable questions. He told the Goths that "the quarrel between the different parties was really one of personal rivalry and involved no difference in doctrine." Since the Roman emperor at the time was on the Arian side, it would be all the better if the Goths were on the same side.[9]

Meanwhile, as ugly as the Arian dispute was getting, it couldn't begin to match the ugliness of imperial politics. Constantine II and that other brother, the son of the late Constantine the Great whom we haven't yet mentioned, Constans, never got along very well. In 340, their long dispute erupted into open war. Constantine was killed. And then there were two: Constantius in the East, and the not-very-well-liked Constans in the West.

One advantage the West had, though, was that it was not agitated by the Arian controversy the way the East was.

Councils Everywhere

Nicaea was supposed to have settled everything, but obviously it hadn't. Constantius was firmly on the Arian side by this point. And between the extremes were various attempts at making a compromise position—something that would satisfy both sides by papering over the major differences, or just refusing to talk about them.

To the West, all this agitation in the East looked like madness. And it especially looked like madness when exiled bishops from the East started showing up in Rome and other cities of the West.

Pope Julius, watching these exiles flow into Rome, decided the time had come to write a half-angry, half-pleading letter to the Eastern bishops who were responsible for all this exiling.

"O dearly beloved," he wrote, "the decisions of the Church are no longer according to the Gospel, but tend furthermore to banishment and death!"[10]

Even if the charges against all these bishops were true, this was not the way to handle them, said Pope Julius. If bishops of apostolic churches such as Alexandria are accused, the pope in Rome should be consulted.

"And why was nothing written to us concerning the church of the Alexandrians in particular? Are you not aware that the custom has been for word to be written first to us, and then for a just sentence to be passed from this place?"[11]

For the Eastern bishops to take it upon themselves to punish a fellow bishop was against both tradition and canon law. "This is a different form of procedure, and this practice is new. I beg you, bear with me willingly. What I write is for the common good. What we have received from the blessed Apostle Peter, that I signify to you."[12]

And still the controversy continued. The pagan historian Ammianus Marcellinus blamed Constantius for most of it. "He confused the Christian religion, which is plain and simple, with old women's superstitions, in investigating which he preferred to perplex himself rather than settle its questions with dignity, so that he excited much dissension—which he further encouraged by diffuse, wordy explanations."[13]

Ammianus says that Constantius called so many councils that he bankrupted the imperial transit system, which was supposed to be for government use only, but which he placed at the service of the bishops every time he summoned them to yet another meeting. "He ruined the establishment of public conveyances by devoting them to the service of crowds of priests, who went to and fro to different synods, as they call the meetings at which they try to settle everything according to their own fancy."[14]

Constantius, in fact, was becoming more and more of an Arian bigot. He seems to have relished an intellectual battle, but he was poorly armed for it. His Arian hangers-on played on his suspicion and superstition whenever they saw a way of gaining an advantage for their side. One of them, Valens, bishop of Mursa, came up with a clever way to make himself look authoritative to Constantius. As a battle was raging, Valens planted a line of messengers along the road, so that news could be relayed to him almost instantly. Then he reported the victory to Constantius before anyone else knew about it, explaining that the news had been brought to him by an angel. Apparently Constantius believed him.[15]

All this must have been alternately amusing and appalling to the pagans who remained in the Empire. But they were probably not amused when Constantius announced an end to Constantine's policy of toleration.

Constantius Consolidates

"Superstition shall cease," Constantius grandly decreed in 341. "The madness of sacrifices shall be abolished." He went on to declare that anyone who offered sacrifices in violation of his edict would suffer "a suitable punishment." The fact that he didn't specify the punishment may be an indication that Constantius didn't expect this edict to be enforced strictly. A pagan governor might decide that a suitable punishment was a wink.[16]

The next year, Constantius and his brother Constans issued a joint edict that temples outside the walls of Rome should be preserved. We can guess that the same policy was followed for other cities. It was still technically illegal to offer sacrifices, but temples that provided "certain plays, or spectacles of the circus, or contests" were allowed to keep entertaining people in the traditional way. In practice, the suburban temples probably kept going much as before, with diminishing congregations.

Some pagans might have remarked that the real spectacle of the circus was at the top of the Christian Church. The pagan historian Ammianus Marcellinus remarked acidly that no wild animal is as much of a danger to mankind as one Christian is to another, which tells us what an unedifying spectacle the whole Arian controversy had become.[17]

The zealous Arian faction was a small minority, but one that had enormous power because the emperor of the East was on its side. The majority clung to the idea that Christ, the Son of God, was truly God, not a created being. A substantial waffling middle favored one side and then the other—some looking to back the winner, but many driven by a real desire for peace among Christians.

An indication of how changeable the political landscape was in those days is that in 346, with Constantius still firmly in power, Athanasius made another triumphant return from exile.

In the West, Constans still favored the orthodox faith. But, as often happened in Roman history, one of the legions proclaimed another man, Magnentius, emperor. Inevitably the usurper had to fight Constans, and Constans died in the battle. Constantius then refused to accept the usurper as his partner in empire, which meant that another fight was brewing.

There was also the Persian frontier in the East to worry about. So Constantius decided to call up his young cousin Gallus. The sickly boy who had survived the general massacre of the other cousins and uncles was now a relatively healthy young man. He and his little brother Julian had spent their young lives in comfortable but closely watched retirement in the country. Now Gallus was suddenly told he was being made Caesar. He had an authority second only to that of Constantius, and he was responsible for keeping the Eastern frontier safe while Constantius mopped up in the West.

Constantius did win the war against Magnentius, which made him undisputed Augustus of the whole Roman Empire—both East and West—like his father before him. What the West noticed most about the change was that now there was an Arian emperor in charge. And he was a compulsive meddler in Church affairs.

By this time, along with most of the extreme Arian party, Constantius had determined that his number-one enemy was Athanasius. And now that he was in control of the West, he had the bishop of Rome within his jurisdiction as well. If Athanasius were to be condemned by the pope, then Constantius and his Arian friends would win their hearts' desire.

In 352, the strong-willed Julius died, and his replacement as bishop of Rome was a good Christian named Liberius who didn't quite have Julius's iron constitution. Constantius decided that Liberius was his opportunity and pressured him mercilessly for a condemnation of Athanasius.

To his credit, Liberius refused. Although Constantius had managed to bully a bunch of Eastern bishops into condemning Athanasius, Liberius had heard from a larger number who supported the beleaguered bishop of Alexandria. He didn't trust the evidence against Athanasius, he said. It required quite a bit of bravery from the poor man to write to the emperor of the world in those terms, and he probably knew before he sent his letter that Constantius would be furious.

Constantius didn't give up. He called councils to condemn Athanasius. When any bishops refused to vote his way, he threatened them with exile. "My will is canon law!" he roared at one council of Western bishops. "The bishops of Syria put up with it when I make these pronouncements, and you will, too!"[18]

Liberius held out, so the emperor gave him a choice: agree, or it's exile in Thrace. Liberius picked Thrace.

Having gotten what he considered a valid condemnation of Athanasius from compliant bishops—all the others having been either exiled or kept away from the councils—Constantius tried to have Athanasius arrested.

Athanasius was in church for a night vigil when five thousand soldiers suddenly surrounded the building. The general in charge, Syrianus, ordered them not to let anyone get past them. Athanasius calmly sat on the bishop's throne and directed the deacon to read a psalm and the congregation to give the responses.

When it became clear that Athanasius wasn't coming out, Syrianus and his soldiers broke in.

Now there was panic. People were running everywhere, and the clergy shouted to Athanasius to escape. He refused. He shouted back that they should go first: he would wait until he had seen everyone else out safely. And he sat while the panicked congregation ran this way and that—the soldiers, knowing their target, seem to have let everyone else go. But then, just as the church was mostly clear, a couple of the clergy grabbed hold of Athanasius (who was a very small man) and carried him bodily out of the church. Somehow they managed to slip by the soldiers in the confusion. And no one was hurt.[19]

So Athanasius went into his third exile. It's a mark of how deeply popular he was in Alexandria that the general Syrianus thought it would take five thousand soldiers to arrest him—and that even with that number he failed.

Julian Rising

Meanwhile, the East was claiming Constantius's attention again. Gallus had failed as Caesar. Given almost unlimited authority, he didn't know quite what to do with it, and he seems to have used it mostly for parties. Constantius got rid of him by having him executed for treason. Then, a year later, he made Gallus's brother, Julian, Caesar in the West.

No one had expected Julian to amount to anything. He had spent all his time among old books. "Some men have a passion for horses, others for birds, others again for wild beasts; but I from childhood have been infused with a passionate longing to acquire books."[20] Julian loved all the old stories from Greek and Roman mythology, and he had read all the standard military classics. His favorite was Julius Caesar's *Gallic War*, which was full of good advice about fighting barbarians in Gaul.

But Julian had no military experience at all. When Constantius summoned him, he was in Athens, completing his university education. His fellow students thought he was a bit odd: he would fall into fits of intellectual enthusiasm, shaking all over, his head jerking this way and that, his thoughts pouring out in a jumble. But he was clever. They could see that.

In Athens, Julian was in the best intellectual company. It was the ancient equivalent of the Ivy League or Oxbridge. Julian had enjoyed getting to know talented students like the intense young fellow named Basil from Cappadocia and his more easygoing friend Gregory, both of whom were hard to keep up with in rhetoric class. And of course he enjoyed just being there in Athens, where so much of Greek history, myth, and thought had originated. Very few, in fact, realized just how much he was enjoying it.

He was then snatched from Athens and carted off to Gaul to be Caesar—a job that had already proved fatal to his elder brother. He had to give up his pursuit of philosophy to look like a soldier. That was all that was expected of him—most of the managing of the army would be in the hands of Constantius's trusted minions. The army just needed a Caesar to look up to.

Constantius never expected that Julian would actually start making important military decisions. And he certainly didn't expect Julian to be good at it. Constantius was a suspicious type by nature, and it can't have made him comfortable to hear the reports coming in from the West. But soon, Julian raided Germany—a splendid victory. Then Julian sent a thousand captured Frankish warriors with his compliments to his cousin. Julian even sorted out revenue problems in Gaul; all seemed to be running smoothly now. It looked as though Julian was making himself too popular in Gaul. He might even have to be eliminated like Gallus.

But Constantius had the whole Church to deal with. He had the same goal as his father, Constantine: unity. The difference was that Constantine had taken the Church as he found it. When there were questions of theology to sort out, he called the bishops together and had them do the sorting. Then he accepted their decision. Constantius, instead, answered the questions himself and demanded that the bishops agree with him. He was making himself head of the Church as well as the secular government, and woe to anyone who got in the way.

Constantius was more and more insistent on rejecting *homoousios* ("consubstantial") in the Nicene Creed in favor of saying that the Son was *homoios*—"like" the Father. While the Arians could easily accept that, the orthodox Catholics could not. When the Arians said "like," they meant that the Son was definitely subordinate to the Father, a position they—and Constantius—insisted on. The extremists, knowing that the emperor was on their side, were abandoning the pretense that they accepted the Nicene Creed.

A lot of pride was bound up in the cause, and a lot of money and property, too. The problem seemed insurmountable. Between the extremes, a compromise party suggested *homoiousios*—"of like being," a Greek word that differed from *homoousios* by only one *iota*, the smallest letter in the Greek alphabet. But the compromise didn't satisfy many—certainly not Constantius, who exiled *homoiousian* bishops as readily as he did *homoousian* bishops. But Constantius's severity only made the party lines harden.

At last, in Gaul, the expected happened. Julian's soldiers proclaimed him Augustus, and the long-veiled hostility between Julian and Constantius headed for open civil war.

But just before the inevitable clash of armies, Constantius suddenly fell sick and died. As his last acts, he was baptized—like his father, he had put off baptism till near death—and willed the Empire to his cousin Julian. There would be no civil war.

There would, however, be a few changes. Julian arrived at Constantinople as fast as the famous Roman roads could carry him. But the news had probably arrived faster. As soon as he heard that Constantius was dead, Julian stopped his public pretense of being a Christian and revealed that he was a pagan.

YOU BE THE JUDGE:

None of the early councils of the Church were about the Eucharist. Doesn't that indicate that no one believed in the Real Presence of Christ until much later?

It's true that the councils held in Nicaea, Ephesus, Constantinople, and Chalcedon did not address the matter of the Real Presence of Christ in the Eucharist. But that's not because nobody believed that the Eucharist really *is* the Body and Blood of Christ.

To the contrary, *everyone* believed it, and that's why no councils addressed the issue.

The Church only defines what is disputed. When something doesn't need to be clarified, the Church tends to leave well enough alone. It's clear that Christians believed that Christ is present in the Eucharist from the beginning. We see powerful testimony to this in the letters St. Ignatius of Antioch wrote while traveling to his execution in Rome. The doctrine appears also in the works of St. Justin Martyr, St. Irenaeus, St. Hippolytus, St. Ambrose, St. Augustine, St. Cyril of Jerusalem, St. John Chrysostom, and many others. We also see that Christians, when accused of cannibalism by their pagan neighbors, did not defend themselves by saying that what they were consuming was only a symbol.

Chapter 6

The Counterrevolution

Beautiful Daphne: the jewel of the East, vacation spot of the rich and famous, Antioch's most fashionable suburb. It was as lush and beautiful as its reputation promised, and the young emperor Julian eagerly looked forward to the impressive ceremonies at the temple of Apollo.

At last he would see the very spot where unwilling Daphne, pursued by the god Apollo, had been changed into a laurel and thus escaped his clutches. Of course, as an enlightened and reasonable pagan, Julian understood that under the veil of the myth lay a deep and meaningful mystery about . . . something. But he had longed to see this spot ever since he first heard the story or read about it in one of his books. Julian had previously sent instructions to have the neglected temple repaired and restored, and the city council of Antioch knew he was coming. Such a wealthy metropolis could afford to put on a magnificent spectacle for him.

What a sight it would be! After decades of neglect, the cult of the god Apollo could at last be revived in all its accustomed splendor. There would be a colorful procession to the temple, with everyone dressed in their finest festival outfits. There would be a long line of sacrificial animals, gallons of wine for libations (and more for the participants, of course), and those delicious honey cakes. There would be incense to fill the air with its sweetness, and choirs singing those good old hymns to Apollo. Perhaps a choir would be out in full force in their splendid white robes.

But it was all much too quiet as Julian and his entourage approached the temple. The temple itself still appeared tatty, although there was a prosperous-looking church right beside it. And where were the choirs singing hymns? Where were the lowing and bleating sacrificial animals? Where were the young men in white and the reverent crowds of worshipers?

The only sound was the occasional honking of a solitary goose.

"Where are the sacrifices?" Julian asked.

No answer.

"Where is the incense? Where are the singing choirs? Where are the honey cakes?"

Still no answer.

"Where is the *priest*?"

At last a little old man came from behind the shrubbery, towing a honking goose on a rope.

"I am the priest," the man answered as bravely as he could.

"Were you waiting for me to begin?" Julian asked, and the goose honked again. "Was I supposed to give the signal?"

"The signal?" the old priest asked confusedly as the goose honked.

"For the sacrifices! For the festival of the god! Where are the sacrificial animals?"

"Well," said the priest (and the goose honked), "I . . . um . . . have this goose."

Julian stood mute for a moment, his mouth hanging open. Then he pulled himself together, with a calm that made most of his entourage cringe, and demanded, "And is this *goose* what the people of the great city of Antioch considered appropriate for this solemn festival?"

"No, this is my goose," the priest replied. "I brought it from home. The city, um, didn't prepare anything." The old man shuffled from one foot to the other and looked at the ground. At last he added, "But we can sacrifice my goose together if you like."

The goose honked.[1]

I've only elaborated the details of this story a little. This account follows closely Julian's own narration of the incident. Julian is, in fact, the most thoroughly self-documented of all Roman emperors, and much of what we know about him is told to us in his own words.

The Lure of the Golden Age

For years Julian had envisioned a restored Roman Empire that had returned to its roots. It would be the Empire of Augustus: strong, prosperous, virtuous, and faithful to the gods who had made Rome great in the first place.

Of course, this golden age existed only in Julian's vivid imagination. The Empire in Augustus's time had been prosperous, but the gods were in disrepute, and the upper classes spent most of their time undermining each other and breaking up each other's marriages. But it was a beautiful picture in Julian's mind. And when he became emperor, he determined that he would make his Empire match the picture.

Julian had gotten most of his knowledge of the world from books. He really had no other option. His cousin Constantius had kept him safely in exile most of his young life; he had lived in enviable luxury, but until a few years before he became emperor, he hadn't been allowed to go anywhere or do anything.

So he concentrated on his education. He was a very good student. And the pagan classics were the basis of a liberal education, even in these Christian times. Julian had a Christian education—even as a pagan emperor, he could quote Christian scripture when it suited him. But it was the pagan curriculum that really captured him. He was intrigued by philosophy, and he read all he could and learned all he could. But mythology held even more fascination for him. He was seduced by superstition.

It seems that not all the priests of the pagan mystery cults were entirely honest and straightforward. They made use of the kind of illusions a vaudeville magician might have in his bag of tricks, passing them off as the actions of an easily amused god. These bogus miracles were effective in duping the gullible, and for all his education, Julian proved very gullible.[2]

Julian was initiated into the pagan mystery cults one after another. He built up quite a collection of them. His favorite seems to have been the cult of Cybele, whose rituals literally whipped her worshipers into a frenzy. The whip, in fact, was one of her symbols. Lucian of Samosata has left us an uncomfortably vivid description of the Day of Blood, as Cybele's big festival was called. On the day of the festival, he tells us, a crowd came together at the temple of the goddess. The Galli, as Cybele's priests were called (they wore women's clothing and ornaments), celebrated the mysteries, while the crowds grabbed whips and started lashing each other's backs. All this was accompanied by a racket of flutes and pounding percussion.

"These days," Lucian adds, "the Galli are increasing. For whenever the Galli play the flutes and celebrate the mysteries, at once the mania enters many, for there are certainly many who have come." And what happens when the "mania" enters someone? "And I'll tell you what they do. Some young man touched by the madness throws off his clothes with a great shout, goes into the middle, and picks up a sword. (I think a number of them have been set up in preparation.) Grasping it, he mutilates himself forthwith."[3]

Once the young man had castrated himself, he ran into the street and threw the amputated parts into some house, which was then obliged to give him women's clothing. From then on, he was one of the Galli. Presumably some slave cleaned up the mess.

Yes, Julian was a big fan of philosophy, but it would be hard to say that was the primary attraction of paganism for him.

Publicly, though, during his university days in Athens, Julian had conformed to Christianity. One of his pagan friends, the historian Ammianus Marcellinus, remembered those days of secrecy in terms of Aesop's old fable about the ass disguised in a lion's skin. Julian, he said, was a lion who had disguised himself in an ass's skin. It was a particularly pointed remark because the ass was a well-known symbol of insult against Christians. The earliest known visual representation of Christ's crucifixion is actually an anti-Christian graffito in Rome: it shows a man on his knees worshiping a crucified man with an ass's head.

Whatever his personal views of Christians, though, Julian had decided that he would not be a persecutor. He would stick to Constantine's policy of toleration.

That would prove a lot more difficult than he thought it would be.

Up Close and Personal:

ST. BASIL THE GREAT

St. Basil played a key role in the development of Catholic social teaching. Charitable practices and institutions were well established in the Church by the time he was born in 329, and everyone knew the scriptural exhortations to kindness and hospitality. But Basil was perhaps the first to consider these scriptures in a systematic reflection and apply them to problems in society.

Basil received an excellent secular education. His father, a respected professor of rhetoric, was his first teacher. He pursued later studies in Athens and Constantinople. Among his classmates were a future emperor and other renowned public figures.

But Basil withdrew from the world and established a monastic community. Even then, social concerns were a recurring theme in his writings. The ideal monk, he said, is one whose prayer is augmented by work—work done so that "they may have something to distribute to those in need."

Named bishop of Caesarea in Pontus, Basil insisted upon the Church's rights against the encroaching state. He refused to be intimidated by the emperor Valens, who was a heretic. And he frustrated the ambitions (and vanity) of his governor, who complained, "Never have I been spoken to with so much liberty." To which Basil replied, "Maybe that's because you've never met a bishop." In his constant vigilance for the Church's freedom, Basil served as a model for bishops in all ages.

He clearly affirmed the universal equality of human beings before God: "To every man belongs by nature equality of like honor with all men, and . . . superiorities in us are not according to family, nor according to excess of wealth, nor according to the body's constitution, but according to the superiority of our fear of God." Nor, he said, should one tribe or nation claim advantage over another: "The saints do not all belong to one country. Each is venerated in a different place. So what does that imply? Should we call them city-less, or citizens of the whole world? Just as at a common meal those things laid before the group by each are regarded as available to all who meet together, so among the saints, the homeland of each is common to all, and they give to each other everywhere whatever they have to hand" (Basil, Homily 338.2).

Basil's doctrine was concretized in the construction of the campus known as the Basileidas, which included a soup kitchen, poorhouses, a trade school, a hostel for needy travelers, personal care for the elderly, and a hospice for the dying. His staff of male and female ascetics dispensed food and medical care to all who came, regardless of their religious affiliation. The duty to serve the poor, however, applied to all Christians. In appealing to the rich, Basil often emphasized that it was in their own best interest to aid the poor, as they would be judged worthy of heaven based on the charity they demonstrated on earth.

Freedom of Religion—Sort Of

As emperor, Julian immediately decreed freedom of religion for all, pagan and Christian. And he also decreed that the pagan temples were to be restored.

That was where he first ran into trouble. Many of the pagan temples—which had been crumbling even before Constantine's conversion—had been torn down, taken over, or converted into churches. Even if the bricks had been used in a church or a private house, however, Julian's order demanded that those bricks go back into a restored pagan temple. The chaotic results were immediately obvious in Constantinople, where, on Julian's orders, several churches were demolished to restore the pagan temples of old Byzantium. Constantine's city had been built without any new temples at all, and many of the already-abandoned temples in the old town of Byzantium had been torn down to be recycled into churches.[4]

Some had been turned into private houses. Even some of Julian's pagan friends found themselves on the wrong side of this edict. His great admirer, the orator Libanius, had to beg Julian for indulgence for his own relatives who had made houses out of disused temples. After all, it had been done in a completely legal way—the policy of Constantius, you know. It wasn't their fault.[5]

And unlike Constantine, who had thought through those problems when he demanded that confiscated property be returned to Christians, Julian had made no provision for imperial compensation to people who had legally bought property and now were forced to hand it over.

Just the logistics of sorting out who owned what were hard enough. But inevitably, pagans used the new imperial favor as an excuse to settle old scores. Julian reiterated more than once that he did not intend any harm to come to the Christians—or "atheists" or "Galileans," as he always called them—but that didn't mean a governor with a grudge, or a mob with pitchforks and torches, wouldn't give a more expansive interpretation to his decrees.[6]

At first, Julian tried to make a show of broad-mindedness by including prominent Christians in his government—notably his old college chum Basil, who had gained a reputation as one of the most prominent intellectuals in the East. Basil refused, however. He had recently founded a monastic community in his home city of Caesarea in Cappadocia, and he had big plans for it.

And Julian's show of evenhandedness concealed a broader plan. Although he insisted that Christians were not subject to penalties, he had a not-very-secret hope that he could cure his Empire of the Christian disease in a short time.

One piece of his clever plan was to bring back all the Christians who had been exiled for being the wrong kind of Christian. Athanasius, for example, was allowed to return to Alexandria. It sounded very fair and tolerant, but it had the effect Julian had hoped for: it created confusion and unrest in every Christian diocese.

Pretty soon, though, Julian revealed his true interests and began openly favoring pagans. "I declare by the gods that I do not want the Galileans to be put to death, or unjustly beaten, or to suffer anything else; but I still emphatically maintain that those who reverence the gods must be preferred to them."[7]

Soon he issued an edict that officers in the city police must offer pagan sacrifices. Those who didn't offer the sacrifice could still be in the police force, but they would be demoted.

And then came what Julian's biographer Adrian Murdoch called his "master stroke." Julian took over the education business. He declared that Christians could no longer teach grammar, rhetoric, or philosophy—the foundations of education. Let them have their St. Paul, he said. But how can they teach the old myths if they don't believe in them?

At once, he took Christianity out of the educational system altogether. It would be like a modern law saying that Christians couldn't teach math and science. Let them have their book of Genesis if they're so attached to it. They can teach from that.

Julian also attacked the cult of the martyrs. Pagans had a horror of dead bodies, whereas Christians revered the relics of the martyrs. Julian decreed that no burials could take place during the day (so that pagans wouldn't be disgusted by seeing the corpses). And bodies of martyrs all over the Empire were dug up and either removed or destroyed.

So it was becoming obvious that Christians were second-class citizens. They weren't persecuted, but if Julian had his way, the Galilean disease would fade away in a generation or two. And paganism ought to flourish.

But it didn't.

Real pagan religion had long since died as a vital force. Even before Constantine, it was a corpse on life support. When the government subsidies dried up, so did pagan worship.

And Julian's idea of paganism was a fantasy. It had never really existed. In fact, Julian was instinctively Christian, and his reaction to the

Christians he knew (all the Christians in his family were Arians, by the way) was founded on Christian feeling.

Like Constantius, Julian imagined himself as head of the Church—but it would be a pagan church. And there had never been a pagan "church." There had never really been such a thing as "paganism." There had only been a spectrum of individual cults and collections of colorful stories. Certainly the dispirited remnants of those cults didn't know how to form themselves into a coherent church. And they didn't really want to.

And they were completely baffled when Julian tried to teach them charity.

Christianizing Paganism

"The Hellenic religion does not prosper as I desire, and it is the fault of those who profess it," Julian wrote one day to his pagan bishop of Galatia, Arsacius the high priest. "For the worship of the gods is on a splendid and magnificent scale, surpassing every prayer and every hope."[8]

Of course, the only reason for that splendor and magnificence was that, through his imperial donations, Julian had been pumping blood into the rotting corpse of paganism. There was no life in it otherwise. But Julian was confident that he knew the answer to that problem.

"Why, then, do we think that this is enough? Why do we not observe that it is their benevolence to strangers, their care for the graves of the dead, and the pretended holiness of their lives that have done most to increase atheism?" (By "atheism," Julian meant Christianity, of course—a common charge of pagans, since Christians denied the existence of ancient gods.) "I believe that we ought really and truly to practice every one of these virtues. And it is not enough for you to practice them, but so must all the priests in Galatia, without exception."

We can imagine Arsacius's jaw dropping as he read this letter. His boss had just told him that he wasn't acting enough like a Christian.

But Julian saw that it was the Christians' way of life that made them so good at converting pagans. He thought of it as a sort of conspiracy. "It is my opinion that when the poor came to be overlooked by the priests, the impious Galileans noticed it and devoted themselves to this kind of philanthropy," he wrote on another occasion.[9] He compared the Christians to creepy slave-catchers who lure children with sweet cakes and then bundle them off to a foreign slave market.

And Julian had a plan for Arsacius to follow: "In every city establish frequent hostels in order that strangers may profit by our benevolence. I do not mean for our own people only, but for others also who are in need of money. I have just now made a plan by which you may be well provided for this: for I have given directions that 30,000 *modii* of grain shall be assigned every year for the whole of Galatia, and 60,000 *sextarii* of wine. I order that one-fifth of this be used for the poor who serve the priests, and the remainder be distributed by us to strangers and beggars."[10]

You'll notice that Julian doesn't expect pagan worshipers to provide any of this bounty; he has an imperial budget for it. The Christian Church had created a whole network of social services while it was still a persecuted underground cult, but Julian knows the pagans well enough not to expect that to happen even in the sunshine of imperial favor.

Still, Julian hopes his idea will counter the conspiracy of the Christians. "For it is disgraceful that, when no Jew ever has to beg, and the impious Galileans support not only their own poor but ours as well, all men see that our people lack aid from us."[11]

You see how clever those Galileans are? They support the poor just because they're poor, whether they're Christian or not. Whereas pagans can't even support their own poor, let alone the Christian poor.

The old cults had never been centers of charity. That wasn't the way they worked. Pagan gods had operated on a simple quid-pro-quo system. You gave the gods the sacrifices and worship they required, and the gods didn't fling thunderbolts at you or wipe out your navy in a storm. This business of feeding the poor and doing good to your enemies was . . . well, *Christian* was the only word for it.

But it was the way Julian's imaginary golden age had worked. "Teach those of the Hellenic faith to contribute to public service of this sort, and the Hellenic villages to offer their first fruits to the gods; and accustom those who love the Hellenic religion to these good works by teaching them that this was our practice of old."[12]

All in all, there's no better demonstration of what Christianity had actually accomplished than the short reign of Julian the Apostate, as history remembers this strange, pedantic young man who found himself emperor. The Christians had changed the mental landscape of the whole world. It was no longer possible to imagine being "religious" without caring for the poor, the sick, and the stranger. Even pagans were thinking Christian thoughts. A new moral ideal had come into the world: love your neighbor as yourself. And once it had come in, not even the most powerful man in the world could pry it out of his own head.

But it wasn't an ideal that the old pagan cults accommodated very well. The pagans simply weren't competent to make Julian's mirror image of Christian virtue a reality. As for the Christians, they just laughed at him—especially in Antioch, a city that Julian never forgave as long as he lived.

Which wasn't very long.

There's not much more to Julian's story. He decided that Rome needed a splendid victory over the Persians, and he led his army deep into Persia, using the tactics he had learned from so many books of military history. The Persians were too smart for those. In 363, two years into his reign, Julian was killed by a spear from an unknown enemy.

An old legend says that his last words were, "You win, Galilean."

Chapter 7

The Christian Empire
and Beyond

Imagine yourself visiting Caesarea in Cappadocia. It looks a lot like any other Eastern Roman city of the later 300s: massive public buildings, splendid new churches (especially the bishop's new church, which is quite a marvel), a colorful market with vendors hawking goods from as far away as China, soaring aqueducts, and all the other things that make a Roman city impressive.

You fall into conversation with one of the locals and compliment him on all you've seen so far.

"Oh, yes," he replies. "It's a nice-enough town as towns go. But have you seen the *New* City?"

"The New City?" you repeat.

"Come on," your new friend says, bursting with civic pride. "I'll show you."

The New City

"Go out a little way from the city," St. Gregory Nazianzen wrote, describing Caesarea, "and have a look at the New City—the warehouse of piety, the common treasury of the wealthy, where their extra riches—yes, and even their necessities—are stored, because of his exhortations."[1]

Whose exhortations? Gregory was talking about his old friend Basil, the one who had refused a position in Julian's government because he had better things to do.

Now, in our imaginary visit to Caesarea, we can see what those better things are. Here, on a pleasant suburban tract of land, is a complex of buildings freshly put up to take care of all the people pagan society had never thought of taking care of.

One of the buildings is a hostel for travelers who can't afford to stay at an inn—or who don't want to mingle with the drunks and prostitutes who are part of the usual social landscape of inns in the Roman Empire. There's also a poorhouse for the homeless, a retirement home for the elderly who have no one to take care of them, an orphanage, a home for lepers, and a hospital—a place where the sick can not only be housed, but also receive professional medical care from real physicians and round-the-clock tending from staff nurses. This hospital thing is a new idea: as far as we can tell, no one before the fourth century had ever thought of it. Basil (and other similarly minded Christians) had to invent it.

To staff all these institutions, there are monks on site who have dedicated their lives to the work. Other monks might retreat from the world, but to Basil that was missing half the point of the Christian life. "Now the solitary life has one goal," he wrote: "the service of the needs of the individual. But this is plainly in conflict with the law of love, which the apostle fulfilled when he sought not his own advantage but that of the many, that they might be saved."[2] And if you live alone, he explained, you can't devote yourself to good works as efficiently as a community can. When you visit the sick, you're not welcoming strangers; when you feed the hungry, you're neglecting something else. But a community can do all those things at once. "Who, then, would choose the idle and fruitless life in preference to the fruitful life lived according to the commandment of the Lord?"[3]

But what had happened to that talented young student of rhetoric Julian had known in Athens? Why had he turned from studying the classics to taking care of lepers?

It was a woman who changed him. Specifically, his sister.

A Big Sister's Legacy

Like college students everywhere and at all times, Basil was full of himself when he graduated. Fortunately, he had an elder sister who—like elder sisters everywhere and at all times—knew how to cut him down to size.

"Macrina's brother Basil the Great came back from his long studies already an expert orator. He was puffed up past the limit with oratorical pride, and he looked down on the dignitaries of the place. In his own opinion he was far above all the movers and shakers."[4]

That was how Basil's own brother, Gregory of Nyssa (not to be confused with his college friend Gregory Nazianzen), remembered Basil when he came back from Athens to Cappadocia. And it was true that Basil was prodigiously talented. His high opinion of himself was justified. But it must have been annoying.

It seems that Macrina knew just what to do to pop his balloon. Their brother Gregory doesn't tell us exactly what she did, but by the time she was through with Basil, his whole outlook on life had changed. He "turned his back on the glories of this world and despised the fame that comes from rhetoric."[5] Instead, he went to work.

Like many Christians of his time, Basil had remained a catechumen and put off baptism. But now he had himself baptized, signaling that he was ready to devote his life to Christ. And then he went on tour.

His object was to see how the monastic movement had developed in Syria, Palestine, and especially Egypt. If he was going to devote his whole life to Christ, he wanted to do it right.

The monastic movement certainly had been developing. What had started in the third century with a few men retiring to the Egyptian desert had blossomed into communities of men and women all over the Empire, especially in the East. Some of those communities had thousands of residents; they were effectively new cities. Others were actually built in the midst of cities, as oases of peace and charity amid the bustle.

In ordinary cities in classical times, the family was the support system. If you were sick, hungry, or out of money, your family took care of you. (And if you had no family, then no one took care of you—until the Christians came along.) But entering a monastery meant leaving your family behind. And that meant a new way had to be created to meet the needs of the residents.

What happened was that the monastic community took care of food, shelter, clothing, and health care for its residents. The larger communities did it on an industrial scale, with separate buildings and complete staffs for cooking and laundry, and an infirmary where sick residents were seen by trained physicians and tended day and night.[6]

At first these monastic communities existed mostly for their residents. And many continued that way, as refuges from the world where men or women could lead a contemplative life. (Did you notice that radical little phrase "men or women"? There was almost no difference between communities for men and communities for women—a fact that turned the pagan world's assumptions about the sexes upside down and inside out.)

But many monastics, like Basil, worried that withdrawing from the world left no scope for charity. How could you feed the hungry, give drink to the thirsty, welcome the stranger, clothe the naked, or visit the sick and the prisoners if you didn't go into the world? (See Matthew 25:31–46.)

Or, as Basil himself is said to have put it, "If you live alone, whose feet will you wash?"[7]

Up Close and Personal:

ST. EPHREM OF SYRIA

A deacon, theologian, interpreter of scripture, and writer of hundreds of hymns, Ephrem is the most famous of the Fathers of Syriac Christianity. Most of the well-known Fathers wrote in Greek or Latin, but there were other language traditions in the ancient Church—Syriac, Coptic, Armenian, Ethiopic—and these continue even today. Ephrem saw that many heresies were spread abroad by means of catchy tunes and memorable verse. He sought to use the same methods for teaching the orthodox faith. He took familiar folk tunes and replaced their lyrics with scriptural and catechetical content. He trained a women's choir to sing his songs in the marketplace, captivating all hearers.

Ephrem also advanced the social and charitable mission of the Church. During a time of epidemic, he persuaded local authorities to turn public properties into a sort of infirmary for the sick, indigent, orphaned, and abandoned. Historians see this as one of the first medical facilities dedicated to extended care—an ancestor of the modern hospital.

Within the Catholic Church, Syriac Christianity endures today in the Antiochene and Chaldean liturgical rites and the five distinct churches that belong to them (Maronite, Syriac, Syro-Malankara, Chaldean, and Syro-Malabar).

The Catholic Majority in an Arian World

While Basil built his New City—even in his lifetime, people were calling it the Basileidas, "Basil's Place"—Jovian, who succeeded Julian as emperor, was carefully avoiding favoring any sect. But Jovian lasted only a year. He was succeeded by Valentinian in the West and Valens in the East. Valentinian kept up the policy of neutrality. But Valens was a bigoted Arian, very much in the mold of Constantius.

It wasn't long before Basil was in Valens's sights. Basil had gained quite a reputation, not just by his good works, but also by his theological writings. What made him especially dangerous was that he was reaching out to the middle—the undecideds who thought that maybe the truth lay somewhere between Arius and Athanasius. By sympathetically listening to their concerns, he was gently wooing them for the orthodox Catholic side.

So Valens sent his governor to demand that Basil, who was bishop by now, accept communion with the extreme Arians. If not, the emperor was ready with a decree of exile.

Knowing he was going up against a theological and rhetorical heavy hitter, the governor trod lightly at first. These little squabbles are unimportant in the big scheme of things, he said. Is a minor point of doctrine worth all the trouble? We need to keep up with the times. The emperor will be very pleased if you grant his small request, and think how much good you could do if the emperor were inclined to be generous.

"This is little boys' talk," Basil answered abruptly. "You can lure little boys with prizes that way. But anyone who grew up on divine words won't let go of a single syllable of the divine creed. We're ready to accept any kind of death first."

"But the friendship of the emperor—"

"I think the friendship of the emperor is very valuable if it comes with true religion. Otherwise I say it leads straight to hell."

This was too much for the governor. "You're out of your mind," he declared angrily.

"And I hope I'm always as crazy as this," Basil replied.[8]

That was Basil's answer. Eventually Valens got around to making good on his threat. He had a decree of exile drawn up, but as he started to sign it, the pen broke. So he picked up another pen, but that one broke too. When the third pen broke, Valens tore up the decree. Maybe it was better not to mess with Basil.

In fact, the heavy-handed imperial interference was having exactly the opposite effect from what the emperor intended. The Arians were shooting themselves in their collective foot. The wobbling middle was beginning to wonder, how true can this Arian doctrine be if it has to be imposed by the emperor's will? Maybe the majority is right.

After all, the whole Church had agreed on Nicaea. Basil and Athanasius were standing up for the creed of Nicaea. And they made it clear that Nicaea was a big tent. It had room for a lot of different kinds of Christians.

Battle lines were being drawn, and the battle would be over a stark and simple question: Who controls the Church—the emperor or the bishops?

Constantine had hoped the unity of the Church would unify the Empire. But now it was looking like Church *versus* Empire.

Valens certainly had his weapons in the fight. His pen might not have survived his first attempt to exile Basil, but he could at least undermine the annoying bishop. He took away half of Cappadocia and made it a new province. That meant that Basil, as metropolitan bishop of Cappadocia, instantly lost half the bishops and clergy under his control. Basil fought back by creating new sees and stuffing them with bishops who agreed with him, making up in numbers some of what he had lost in area. Among those bishops were his brother Gregory, who became bishop of Nyssa, and his old friend Gregory Nazianzen, who was assigned to the out-of-the-way town of Sasima. If Valens was going to play hardball, Basil had the equipment.

But Basil's big contribution was in building bridges to create what we might call a Nicene supermajority. The hard-line Arians would never be satisfied with the Nicene Creed, but the *homoiousians*—the people who had worried that *homoousios* might not preserve the distinction between the Father and the Son, but were willing to say that the Son was "of like being"—could be brought around with careful definitions of terms and explanations. The two Gregorys added their considerable talents to the effort. Together, the three of them are remembered as the "Cappadocian Fathers." But only Basil is remembered as "the Great."

Basil must have often felt that he was at a disadvantage. But we can look back now and see that the tide had turned. The silent majority was finding its voice. All over the Christian world, great thinkers were thinking great thoughts.

Some of them were even setting them to music.

The Arians had used catchy songs from the beginning. Arius himself had set his theology—in very bad verse, as Athanasius sneeringly remarked—to a catchy popular tune from the 320s. Perhaps just because the Arians had done it, many of the orthodox Catholic Christians had shied away from musical propaganda.

But way over at the far-eastern frontier of the Empire, a brilliant Syriac-speaking theologian decided it was time to beat the Arians at their own game.

Ephrem (or Ephraim) the Syrian wrote thousands of lines of verse—three thousand, according to Sozomen the historian—that summarized, explained, and upheld the Nicene understanding of Christian theology. Ephrem wrote in his native Syriac, but both his songs and his prose works were translated into Greek and widely circulated. Basil was a great admirer of his work—and, as Sozomen says, "The opinion of Basil, who is universally confessed to have been the most eloquent man of his age, is a stronger testimony, I think, than anything that could be written in his praise."[9]

All that talent had its effect. Ephrem is still remembered as the greatest poet, prose writer, and thinker of the Syriac church. And he was leading the Syriac church in Catholic orthodoxy, giving a voice to the large majority of Syriac-speaking Christians.

As for Basil, he died young. When we look at his huge output of writings, and his equally prodigious New City—and when we hear that he treated many of the lepers and hospital patients himself—it's hard for us to believe that he was only in his forties when he died. Somehow he crammed three or four lifetimes' worth of work into that short period.

When he was dying, it must have seemed to Basil that the victory was a long way off. Exile had finally caught up with him, and though the majority might be with him in the Catholic Church of the apostles, the emperor was still stubbornly Arian. And Athanasius, the tireless champion of Catholic Christianity, was dead. He had managed to come back to Alexandria and be exiled one more time, making a record-breaking five exiles before he finally died. His successor Peter was a committed follower of Athanasius, but no one could replace Athanasius.

Basil couldn't have foreseen how close the Catholic majority was to the victory he had prayed for. Nor could he have foreseen that the victory would begin with a catastrophic defeat.

Victory from Catastrophe

On August 9, 378, the Roman Empire suffered its worst defeat. That was how contemporaries saw it, anyway. One could point to other disasters, with worse casualty numbers, but nothing else had seemed so much like the beginning of the end. At the battle of Adrianople, not only did Gothic barbarians defeat the proud Roman legions (which, incidentally, were almost all made up of barbarian recruits themselves by this time), but they killed the emperor Valens. His body was never recovered; unlike Julian, he didn't even get the compensating dignity of a decent burial.

Things would have been a lot worse if the Romans hadn't been able to regroup under a forceful new emperor named Theodosius. But still, people who lived through that time remembered it as the worst news they had ever heard. For years afterward, they must have asked each other, "Where were you when you heard the news about Adrianople?"

It was "the destruction of the entire globe, the end of the world," wrote the bishop of Milan—a man named Ambrose, of whom we'll hear quite a bit more soon.[10] It seemed as though the almost divine wall of protection that had kept the heartland of the Empire safe from foreign attack had been broken down.

But the silver lining for the Church was that Theodosius, unlike Valens, was a Catholic Christian, devoted to the faith as it was expressed in the Nicene Creed. He was also a baptized Christian by the time he made it to Constantinople. He'd had a health scare, and for a while it looked as if he might die. He didn't, but as a result of the scare he was baptized, and he was determined to take his faith seriously.

In fact, the news had already reached Constantinople before Theodosius did: the new Eastern emperor had announced his intention to lead all his people to the true Catholic faith.

And how would he determine what the true Catholic faith was? That was easy: it was Christianity as professed by Damasus, bishop of Rome, and Peter, bishop of Alexandria.

The pope had always been orthodox. The Arian controversy had been mostly an Eastern affair, except when Arian emperors caused trouble. And Athanasius had always stood for the faith of Nicaea; his handpicked successor was in full agreement with the pope.

Theodosius made it clear what his policy would be as soon as he arrived in Constantinople. The bishop there was an Arian. Theodosius told him he could keep his place if he accepted the Nicene Creed. To his credit, the Arian bishop straightforwardly replied that he couldn't do that.

There was no punishment. But there was no question of his remaining bishop of Constantinople. The Arian services moved to a suburban church outside the city walls. The cathedral was turned over to the large Catholic congregation that had been gathering under the unofficial leadership of Gregory Nazianzen. Gregory found himself suddenly elevated to bishop of Constantinople, in spite of much controversy—he was already bishop of some town in Cappadocia that no one had ever heard of.

The thing is, Gregory hated his new position—and what he hated about it shows how powerful the Church had become in the years since the Edict of Milan. He wrote:

> I wasn't aware that we were supposed to rival the consuls, the governors, the most famous generals, who have no opportunity to be generous with their income—or that our stomachs ought to hunger for enjoying the goods of the poor, and to spend their necessities on luxuries, and belch over the altars. I didn't know we were supposed to ride on splendid horses, and drive in magnificent carriages, and be preceded by a parade and surrounded by applause, and have everyone make way for us as if we were wild animals, and open up a passage so that our approach could be seen from far away.[11]

It was no wonder the position of bishop had been so much coveted by the unscrupulous. The wonder is that so few of the bishops had actually fallen for the worldly trappings of the office. The sheer number of exiles under Constantius and Valens tells the story: most of the bishops remained faithful to the ancient doctrine, even if it meant losing every material thing.

As soon as he had settled in at Constantinople, Theodosius called a council of bishops in the imperial capital. In 381, bishops came together—Catholic and Arian. The debate was open, the emperor said; both sides had the right to speak. But first, a question: "Do you have respect for the teachers who lived before the Church was divided, and are you willing to accept their teachings?"

This was a tough one. The Catholic side answered yes right away. The Arians sensed a trap. They knew in their hearts that it would be hard to find justifications for Arian doctrine in the writings of the earliest Christians. When they eventually had to say, "Um . . . well . . . yes," Theodosius asked them directly, "Will you defer to those teachers as witnesses of Christian doctrine?"

That started the Arians arguing. There was no right answer, and they knew it.

Eventually it was decided that the various factions—Nicene, Arian Lite, and hardcore Arian—should write up statements of their faith.

The emperor himself recommended the adoption of the Nicene statement of faith, and with the Arians dissolving into petty squabbles, most of the bishops there agreed.

Note that there was no bullying. Of course, it was always nice to be on the same side as the emperor. But Constantius and Valens hadn't been able to get their way at councils except by naked threats. The Council of Constantinople was explicitly free to make its own determination. And the creed it accepted is what we know as the Nicene Creed today: the creed of Nicaea, with a few additions from the bishops in Constantinople.

> I believe in one God,
> the Father almighty,
> maker of heaven and earth,
> of all things visible and invisible.
> I believe in one Lord Jesus Christ,
> the Only Begotten Son of God,

born of the Father before all ages.
God from God, Light from Light,
true God from true God,
begotten, not made, consubstantial with the Father;
through him all things were made.
For us men and for our salvation
he came down from heaven,
and by the Holy Spirit was incarnate of the Virgin Mary,
and became man.
For our sake he was crucified under Pontius Pilate,
he suffered death and was buried,
and rose again on the third day
in accordance with the Scriptures.
He ascended into heaven
and is seated at the right hand of the Father.
He will come again in glory
to judge the living and the dead
and his kingdom will have no end.
I believe in the Holy Spirit, the Lord, the giver of life,
who proceeds from the Father,
who with the Father and the Son is adored and glorified,
who has spoken through the prophets.
I believe in one, holy, catholic and apostolic Church.
I confess one Baptism for the forgiveness of sins
and I look forward to the resurrection of the dead
and the life of the world to come. Amen.

YOU BE THE JUDGE:

Didn't Christianity harm the status of women?

In Greco-Roman society, women could not testify in a court of law. They were considered to be unreliable witnesses. They had no self-determination and customarily married the men chosen by their fathers. Literature written by women was scarce in antiquity—almost nonexistent, in fact. And all the epic heroes were warrior males from the aristocracy. Outside Judaism and Christianity, a woman took her identity and security from the males in her life: first her father, then her husband, and finally her sons.

But a quiet revolution took place with the rise of Christianity. The early Fathers condemned the practice of marrying daughters off at an early age. They insisted that women should have vocational freedom—even the choice not to marry and to dedicate themselves in virginity to Christ. Many of the larger-than-life heroes of the early Church were female martyrs: Blandina, Perpetua, Felicity, Agnes, Agatha, Cecilia.

We see this clearly in the first century after the Christian faith was legalized in the Roman Empire. The hospital emerged as an institution for the first time in history, and many of the pioneering hospitals were founded and run by women: Fabiola in Rome, Olympias in Constantinople. Women took to scholarship as well. In Rome, the home of Marcella became a center of scripture study—with training in Greek and Hebrew—and produced the scholars who accompanied St. Jerome in his travels and assisted him in his translations. Women even emerged as popular authors and poets, like Proba in fourth-century Rome.

The greatest saints of the time—Gregory of Nyssa and Augustine of Hippo—did not hesitate to declare themselves the disciples of women. In Augustine's case, it was his mother, Monica. For Gregory, it was his sister, Macrina.

Chapter 8

A Tale of Two Bishops

Milan became the imperial capital of the West. By the late 300s, it was probably bigger than Rome in population, and it was certainly where things were happening. Crusty old Rome had the monuments and the traditions, but it had been losing people for a long time now. Milan had an imperial court and all the prosperity that came with a vast bureaucracy.

And because it had the emperor and his court, it also had a large pocket of Arianism in the otherwise mostly Catholic West. The populace was divided into Arian and Catholic factions. And when Auxentius, the Arian bishop of the place, died, each side was determined that its candidate would be the next bishop of Milan.

It was more than a local question. The bishop of Milan was the emperor's parish priest and confessor. Whoever held the office would have enormous influence over the Western emperor, and specifically over his religious policies.

So the people had gathered in the cathedral to discuss the question of Auxentius's successor. And soon the discussion turned into shouting, and the shouting was beginning to turn into a riot.

Just in time, the governor appeared.

Everyone respected Ambrose the governor. He had always been scrupulously fair to both sides in the Arian controversy. The mob in the church actually quieted down and listened as he begged them not to resort to violence. We're all Christians, he said. Surely, we can choose our bishop with calm deliberation and—

From somewhere in the great church came the voice of a little child: "Ambrose for bishop!"

A few people in the crowd laughed. Ambrose went on with his speech. But then another voice—an adult this time—called out, "Ambrose for bishop!"

And then it dawned on everyone at once that they had hit on the one solution to their bishop problem that didn't involve a brawl. "Ambrose for bishop!" more voices cried, and the shouts became a chant that drowned out the governor's objections.[1]

Ambrose did his best to avoid becoming bishop of Milan. He wasn't even baptized yet. But when a message came in from the emperor Gratian—one of the two Western emperors at the time—congratulating the people of Milan on their wise choice, Ambrose had to give up. Or, more accurately, he was given up by the friend in whose house he was hiding.

So Ambrose was baptized, ordained, and made bishop, and he decided to take his calling very seriously. Although he was a rich man, he got rid of his possessions and used the money to buy nice things for the poor. He only reserved enough to keep his sister in a reasonably comfortable fashion. Then he got down to work and studied theology.

And when he had studied enough, he decided that the time for even-handedness had passed. The Arians were simply wrong. As governor, he could be as tolerant as he liked. But as bishop, it was his duty to teach his flock the truth.

Ambrose was made bishop in 373 or 374. A little more than twenty years later, another great Christian thinker became bishop of Constantinople after having made a reputation in Antioch for his memorable sermons. His name was John, but his preaching was so remarkable that people called him "Golden-Mouthed"—in Greek, *Chrysostom*.

These two bishops both found themselves, much against their will, in charge of the church in one of the imperial capitals. Both ended up knee-deep in imperial politics. Both stood up for what they knew was right against the wrath of emperors. But they came to very different ends. And their two stories show us how the relationship between the Church and the government was diverging in East and West. The two halves of the Empire were headed down different roads.

Ambrose vs. the Pagans

The emperor Gratian, a Nicene Christian, was easy for Ambrose to get along with. But Gratian died in 383, and the Western Empire was left in the hands of the young Valentinian II. Ambrose seems to have decided that he needed to be a strong influence on the young emperor.

We first hear of him giving Valentinian advice in 384. Pagans in the Senate of Rome had sent a petition to have the Altar of Victory, which bore a golden statue of the goddess Victory, restored to the senate house. It had been taken away by Constantius, restored (of course) by Julian, and taken away again by Gratian. Rome was still a very conservative place, and there were still many pagans in the Senate, which was a conservative body even by Roman standards.

The petition had been composed by Symmachus, perhaps the most distinguished orator among the increasingly irrelevant senators. He argued that the old customs had preserved Rome for centuries. The pagan rites had repulsed Hannibal from the walls of Rome; they had kept the Gauls from storming the Capitol.

Ambrose replied to Symmachus's petition point by point. The pagan rites had preserved Rome? They had repulsed Hannibal from the walls? "Hannibal insulted the Roman rites for a long time," Ambrose countered, "and while the gods were fighting against him came right up to the walls of the city to conquer. If the gods were taking up arms to fight for them, why did they let themselves be besieged?"

"And what shall I say about the Senones?" he continued. "The remaining Romans could not have kept them from penetrating the hidden parts of the Capitol if a goose had not betrayed them by its frightened honking. Such protectors the Roman temples have! Where was Jupiter then? Was he speaking in the goose?"

Besides, Ambrose said, Hannibal was praying to the same gods. If they won for the Romans, they lost for the Carthaginians under Hannibal. One way or the other, the old pagan rites lost the war.[2]

The Altar of Victory was not restored.

Ambrose vs. the Arians

About two years after Gratian died, the young emperor Valentinian II declared himself an Arian. So did his very influential mother. And, of course, so did a large number of assorted bureaucrats and hangers-on who deduced that being on the same side of the dispute as the emperor would be good for their careers.

Ambrose had been making great headway in persuading the ordinary Christians of Milan to come back to the Catholic faith. But now there was suddenly a layer of rich and powerful Arians over the mass of ordinary Catholic Christians. The emperor and his mother demanded two of the best churches in Milan for their Arian congregations.

The problem was that the ordinary people in the congregations of these churches didn't want them handed over to the Arians.

Faced with the demand that he relinquish the cathedral to the Arians, Ambrose flatly refused. "A temple of God cannot be handed over by a bishop," he declared.

The congregation roared its approval.

Well, at least the emperor would take the other church. While the people were gathered in the cathedral for Sunday Mass, the news came that imperial officials had taken control of the Portian basilica outside the walls. Immediately, some of the people ran off in that direction, but Ambrose continued with Mass. When he heard that the mob had taken hold of one of the Arian priests, though, he sent his own deacons and priests to rescue the poor man. The Catholics would resist, but he would not have blood spilled.

When representatives came from the emperor, Ambrose explained his position clearly. "I can't hand over the basilica, but I may not fight." He had told the emperor, "The palaces belong to the emperor; the churches to the bishop." And the bishop had no right to give away what he held for the whole Church.

Other bishops had defied emperors before. Some even got away with it. But Ambrose, with his long experience in government, could articulate clearly the principle behind his defiance. The secular government was responsible for the secular sphere of life, and the Church was responsible for the spiritual, and neither one had any right to interfere in the other's responsibilities.

The young emperor threw a predictable tantrum. He called Ambrose a tyrant. He accused his own ministers of collaborating with the bishop: "If Ambrose told you to, you'd bring me to him in chains!" But he failed to evict Ambrose from the churches.[3]

He might have given up, but his mother wouldn't let him. So for months there was a strange state of siege in Milan. Ambrose continued his usual round of visits, prayers at the martyrs' tombs, and ecclesiastical appointments; but he knew that the emperor and his mother were looking for ways to get rid of him. At one point he was apparently ordered to leave Milan and go "wherever you like"—very generous terms of exile. But Ambrose didn't leave, and the emperor didn't dare kick him out by force. In the middle of it all, Ambrose discovered the bodies of hitherto-unknown martyrs and had them transferred to the main basilica, which had the effect of raising the level of popular enthusiasm to a higher pitch than ever.

Every day the people gathered in the basilica to keep watch, knowing that at any moment the emperor might send soldiers to take it over again. Ambrose got them singing to keep their spirits up—a new idea in the Western Church. In addition to his other talents, Ambrose turned out to be a brilliant songwriter.

The sight of so many people gathered in the basilica, cheerfully singing and ready to die in defense of the faith, had a big effect on a certain young man who had traveled to Milan to teach rhetoric. This young teacher would come to have an enormous influence on the Church and the world. Up until that time, he had not been impressed by Christian teachers he'd witnessed or encountered. But Ambrose was of a different order, a man who had all the tricks of rhetoric at his command, but who could also write a song that stuck in your head, and who was willing to give up everything for what he believed in. The young rhetorician started to think these Christians might have something to teach him after all. His name was Augustine, and we'll hear more about him later on.

Eventually, it was Valentinian who gave up. He had too many troubles elsewhere to keep beating his head against the immovable object that was Ambrose. And it wasn't long before his troubles caught up with him. By the year 392, he was dead, leaving Theodosius the sole ruler of the Roman world.

Ambrose and Theodosius

The emperor Theodosius was a Nicene Christian, so we might think that Ambrose would be able to relax a bit. But instead of relaxing, Ambrose worked even harder. The emperor was Catholic—very good. Now Ambrose would help him be the ideal Christian emperor, as far as it lay in his power.

Theodosius was an emperor who was seriously working on the title by which history would know him, "the Great." The historian Adrian Murdoch describes him as "vastly talented,"[4] and most of the writers of his own time seem to agree.

But Theodosius's great fault was a hot temper. He was a sincere Christian and a patriot, but he could be ferocious in his wrath. As emperor, he had the power to turn his wrath into dead bodies.

And the most notorious story about Theodosius involves thousands of dead bodies.

In 390, sports fans in Thessalonica rioted. A certain star charioteer had been put in prison, probably richly deserving it (he had been charged with immorality, and sports stars were much the same then as they are now). In the riot, the military commander of the city was killed.

Theodosius was furious. In his eyes, the whole city was guilty—which, by the way, was consistent with Roman legal theory at the time. He ordered the soldiers to massacre the people. And then he realized what a horrible thing he had done and sent another messenger flying after the first one to cancel the order.

But it was too late. About six thousand people died.

Theodosius felt great remorse for what had happened. But Ambrose demanded more than that of him. He refused the emperor Communion until he did penance in public.

Ambrose explained this in the politest possible way, of course. "Listen, august emperor. I cannot deny that you have a zeal for the faith. I confess that you have the fear of God. But you have a natural vehemence. If it is soothed, you quickly turn it to mercy. If anyone stirs it up, you rouse it so much more that you can hardly restrain it."[5]

It was important to acknowledge the depth of the sin that had been committed, Ambrose said. "A deed has been done in the city of the Thessalonians that has no parallel. I wasn't able to prevent it from happening. I told you it would be a terrible atrocity when I begged you over and over not to do it. And you yourself showed that you thought it was heinous by revoking it too late."[6]

The only way out of sin, Ambrose said, is repentance. "You are a man, and temptation has come upon you. Conquer it. You can only get rid of sin by tears and penitence. Angels can't do it. Archangels can't do it. The Lord himself, the only one who can say 'I am with you' if we have sinned, forgives no one but those who repent."[7]

And the repentance would have to be very public. Ambrose insisted that everyone see Theodosius repenting.

That was what happened. Theodosius might have wondered what the people would think of their emperor when they saw him dressed as a penitent, standing with the other penitents outside Mass.

But he did it.

What did they think? They called him Theodosius the Great.

As for the bishop who made him stand out there, Theodosius gave him his best epitaph: "I never knew a bishop worthy of the name—except Ambrose."

Ambrose set a pattern for strong bishops in the West. With the precedent of Ambrose behind them, Western bishops could make a compelling case that the Church was meant to be independent of secular government.

The bishops in the East wouldn't be so lucky.

Up Close and Personal:

ST. AMBROSE THE SONGWRITER

Ambrose of Milan heard about the music used for worship in the Greek-speaking East, and he decided it was just what the Divine Doctor had ordered for the Latin-speaking West. Ambrose began composing hymns in the Eastern style. They were simple melodies. Their words followed familiar patterns of rhyme and rhythm, so they were easy to remember.

He followed the already established custom of including a verse of doxology in his lyrics. It was usually the concluding verse, and it was dedicated to praise of the Blessed Trinity.

Such content was designed to inoculate his congregations against the Arian heresy—and instill in them an awareness of the most fundamental mystery of Christian faith.

Ambrose's hymns worked. They were so effective at delivering doctrine to memory that his critics accused him of bewitching his congregations.

He found such criticism flattering. He wrote to one correspondent: "They say that the people have been taken in by the charms of my hymns, and certainly I do not deny it. This is indeed a mighty charm and there is none more powerful; for what is more powerful than the confession of the Trinity, cele-brated daily by the voices of the whole people?" (St. Ambrose of Milan, *Sermon Against Auxentius*, 34).

We learn from members of his church that Ambrose used hymns during acts of civil disobedience—to comfort the pro-testers, but also to intimidate the opposing officers of the law. Augustine sang his mother's favorite Ambrosian hymns to con-sole himself after her death.

Watch for the doxology next time you sing an old hymn. Thank St. Ambrose.

The Crisis of the Statues

At just about the time Ambrose was holding down his basilica and holding off the Arians, Antioch was in the grip of a crisis. It was a crisis that would make the reputation of the golden-mouthed priest, John Chrysostum.

The imperial budget was always strained. As government got bigger and more elaborate (remember Julian's ineffective attempt at simplifying it), the wealth of the provinces couldn't keep up. The fact that the rich were experts at avoiding paying taxes didn't help: it left most of the burden on the middle classes and the poor. Meanwhile, the barbarians on the fron-tiers were getting more and more aggressive. Especially after Adrianople, the Empire was straining every resource just to keep the barbarians out—or, increasingly, to keep them quiet once they had been invited in to settle, which was Theodosius's way of dealing with the twin problems of restless barbarians on the outside and depopulated provinces on the inside.

So taxes were going up all the time. And when the emperor imposed yet another special tax, the people of Antioch rioted.

Riots in cities were common throughout the Roman Empire. But things got out of hand when some of the rioters in Antioch—a place that had never taken emperors very seriously (remember how they treated Julian)—pulled down and broke up statues of the emperor and his family.

That was treason. The statues stood for the presence of the emperor. He couldn't be everywhere at once, but in his statue he could be present in cities throughout the Empire. An insult to the statue was an insult to the emperor himself.

When the people of Antioch woke up from their nightmare, they realized what had happened. Certain people were punished by the local government, and maybe they were even the guilty ones. But the common Roman assumption was that the whole city was responsible for an incident like this. Think what happened in Thessalonica a few years later, and you can understand why the people of Antioch were trembling. John Chrysostom remembered that "the greater part of the city had taken refuge from the fear and danger of that occasion" (meaning the "examining," or torturing, of witnesses by the court) "in secret places, in deserts, and in hollows, terror besetting them in all directions; and the houses were empty of women, and the forum of men, and hardly two or three appeared walking together across it—and even these going about as if they were animated corpses."[8] All the people who had relatives under investigation were gathered outside the court, silently praying.

In those fearful days, John preached some of his most famous sermons. He didn't minimize the danger; he urged people to look beyond the present life to the source of all consolation. And there was something comforting about his words. Even if they were going to die, the people felt while listening to John's preaching that they could endure it for the sake of the life to come.

But no one else died. A few of the accused culprits had been executed, but the city was spared—and the story everyone heard was that it was the monks who had saved Antioch.

The emperor Theodosius, hot-tempered as ever, had sent commissioners with instructions to tell the citizens that he was going to burn Antioch to the ground and reduce the Empire's third city to a village. But as the commissioners rode into town, they met a grubby and ignorant monk along the way. They couldn't help meeting him, because he stood in front of them and refused to move until they had heard him. Theodoret tells us that the monk's name was Macedonius, a man who knew nothing about life and lived on the wild mountains. He grabbed the imperial officers by the cloak—not a wise thing to do to officers with the power of life and death—and demanded that they get off their horses and hear what he had to say.

The officers were going to treat him the way they thought he deserved, but some of their escort informed them that this was a well-known holy man, a monk of the wilderness. That was enough. The monks had such a reputation by this time that even imperial commissioners stood in awe of them, no matter how smelly and ignorant they might seem at first glance.

Macedonius told them he had a message for the emperor. "Tell him this: You're not only an emperor. You're also a man. You reign over your fellow men. And man is formed in the image of God. The images that were thrown down have been set up again, and the damage has been repaired. They're as good as new. But if you kill the image of God, how will you ever be able to take back what you've done? How could you bring the people you've killed back to life? How could you restore their souls to their bodies? If one image of bronze is destroyed, we can make as many more as we like. But even you can't make one single hair of someone who's been killed."[9]

The commissioners were impressed enough that they reported the monk's argument word for word to Theodosius. And when he heard it, he had a change of heart. So much so that he even admitted he might have been wrong about the taxes. The thing he had been most angry about, he said, was the way people had treated the statue of his sainted mother. If they had a grievance, they should have taken it out on him alone. But the punishments were revoked, and he was sorry that any blood at all had been spilled.[10]

The golden-mouthed priest reported this wonderful change of heart to his congregation. It capped off a series of some of the most brilliant Christian sermons ever heard. They made John's reputation.

And his reputation brought him nothing but misery.

More Trouble with Statues

Now we flash forward about twelve years. Theodosius was dead by this time, and one of his two useless sons, Arcadius, was the emperor of the East. (The emperor of the West was the even more useless Honorius, whom we'll meet soon.) A new bishop was needed for Constantinople, and who better to preach in the imperial capital than the most famous Christian orator of the time, the one everyone called John the Golden-Mouthed?

John really didn't want to go. He had always wanted to live an ascetic life, a life of self-denial and prayer. And we know from Gregory Nazianzen's description of splendid carriages and endless processions how far the life of Constantinople's bishop was from that ascetic ideal.

Worse than that was the politics. There's a reason we still use the term "byzantine" to describe politics that are shady, underhanded, and infernally complex. That was the way Constantinople worked.

John knew what he was getting into. But he couldn't get out of it. In 398, John Chrysostom was made bishop of Constantinople.

His reputation preceded him, and the crowds who flocked to hear him preach were not disappointed. He was as eloquent as ever.

But John had a problem. He couldn't help telling the truth as he saw it. And what he saw was that the rich were living in luxury while the poor starved. He said so right there in the Church of Holy Wisdom. The poor loved him for it, but the rich were not happy at all.

Most of John Chrysostom's reign as bishop of Constantinople was taken up with one wearying attempt after another to undermine him in the usual subtle Byzantine way.

But the time for subtlety passed when John managed to offend the empress personally.

It was always whispered that Eudoxia was the real power in Constantinople, that Arcadius didn't do a thing without consulting his domineering wife. And the statue of Eudoxia that was erected across from the Church of Holy Wisdom was absurdly expensive. According to the historian Socrates, it was made of silver, and it sat on a base of porphyry.

"At this statue," Socrates says, "they used to hold public celebrations—which John regarded as an insult to the Church. Since he had regained his usual boldness of speech, he used his tongue against those who did these things. Now, although it would have been proper to send a petition to the authorities asking them to discontinue the celebrations, he did not do this, but he employed abusive language and ridiculed those who had enjoined such practices."[11]

The empress took John's sermons as personal insults—and, to be fair, they were pretty insulting. The worst of it was that they were *good*. People laughed and quoted the best lines for days afterward.

John soon found himself in a web of Byzantine politics from which there was no escape. The empress didn't just have him exiled for insulting her; that wasn't the way things were done in Constantinople. Instead, absurd charges were made against him accusing him of all sorts of things, and he was banished to far-off Armenia.

John appealed to the pope in Rome, who took his side. Even the Western emperor Honorius, who seldom took an interest in anything, tried to intervene in his favor. But it was to no avail. When Arcadius and, more importantly, Eudoxia saw that John was corresponding with all these important people from his exile in Armenia, they sent him even farther away, to the other end of the Black Sea. And there, worn out by his troubles and the conditions of his exile, he died.

East and West

As Ambrose was emblematic of the position of Western bishops, John Chrysostom became an emblem for the East. In the West, the bishops successfully stood up for the independence of the Church from the emperor's authority. In the East, the example of John Chrysostom showed that, in a conflict between the bishop and the emperor, the emperor was likely to win.

It didn't matter that St. John Chrysostom's remains were brought back by Theodosius II, the son of Arcadius, thirty years after John died in exile, and that he was remembered after that as one of the greatest figures of the Eastern Church. The precedent had been set. The East would be different from the West.

It was a difference that would last for centuries and shape the history of the Church from then on.

Chapter 9

An Age of Titans

Finally, the Arian battle was almost over in the Roman Empire—although now the Empire was fighting for its life against invading tribes that had been Christianized by Arian missionaries. For the next few decades, the religious landscape would look like that: a Catholic Roman Empire surrounded by Arian barbarians.

That long battle of words over the Arian question of Christ's divinity did have unexpected benefits. It had nurtured a generation of theological titans. The greatest brains in the Empire had applied themselves to the scriptures and the traditions of the apostles, because it was the only way to answer the questions the Arians had raised.

Now a new generation had come up, educated by the greats who had trained in the Arian battleground. The Empire itself might be falling apart, but it would be an age of titans in Christian thought.

A Catholic World

Theodosius had made the Empire officially Christian and Catholic. He was the first emperor to remove all ambiguity: "It is our will that all the peoples who are ruled by the administration of our Clemency shall practice that religion which the divine Peter the Apostle transmitted to the Romans," he decreed soon after he came to the throne.[1] In some ways, it was just a continuation of the policy of Constantius, Julian, and Valens: the emperor gets to decide in matters of religion. Except that there was one enormous difference. Where Constantius had insisted that his will was canon law, Theodosius defined true religion as the religion of the bishop of Rome and the bishop of Alexandria.

About ten years later, Theodosius made pagan religion illegal—and he meant it. There would be no pagan martyrs; the punishments were only fines. But unlike Constantius's edicts, which looked much harsher on papyrus, this law was actually enforced.

Heretics were punished more severely than pagans—their property could be confiscated. It was going to be a Catholic world if Theodosius had anything to say about it.

We can argue about the wisdom of intolerance, but we can say this for Theodosius and the rest of the Christian emperors: they were never as harsh to pagans as pagans had been to Christians. No pagans were thrown to the lions for the entertainment of Christian crowds. No pagans were burned alive to illuminate a mad emperor's garden party. We can say that much for the new order—but we can still allow ourselves a sigh of regret for the quick death of Constantine's brief experiment in religious freedom.

And it is true that Christian mobs were sometimes violent. Mobs are mobs, Christian or not. Some of the more fanatical monks were notorious troublemakers. The pagan rhetorician Libanius—one of Julian the Apostate's most enthusiastic followers, but still active thirty years later—complained to Theodosius about monks who were also ruffians: "They rush to the temples carrying poles, stones, and iron tools, and if they don't have those they use their hands and feet. Then the roofs are knocked in, walls leveled to the ground, images overturned, and altars uprooted—they are a prey to all—while the priests must suffer in silence or die."[2]

Libanius was one of the last notable pagan writers. With or without the tolerance of the emperor, paganism had little life left in it. The greatest writers, the greatest thinkers of the age were almost all Christian.

In fact, Libanius himself may be remembered for some of his speeches, notably his eulogy of Julian the Apostate. But he is much better remembered as the teacher of John Chrysostom, the greatest rhetorician of the generation that followed.

Christian or Ciceronian?

The West also had its rhetoricians. Jerome of Stridon studied in Rome and learned all the tricks of the greatest orators of past centuries. But he was especially enamored with Cicero, the greatest of all Latin orators, whose style is still held up today as the apex of Latin prose, and whose works even now are the usual basis of third-year Latin studies.

Jerome, like many educated Romans, decided to escape the increasingly gloomy and doomed-looking secular world by taking up a religious life. But he took his books with him. They were the one worldly pleasure he couldn't bear to give up.

And then he got sick.

He recalled it years later. He was on his way to Jerusalem to "wage his warfare," as he called his ascetic life, when he came down with a fever. He couldn't sleep; he couldn't eat. He was so ill that his friends began making preparations for his funeral.

In the middle of this struggle, he had a vision.

He saw himself taken up to the judgment seat of Christ. The light was so bright, he remembered, that he couldn't look up: he stood before the Judge with his eyes lowered.

"What kind of man are you?" the Judge asked him.

"A Christian," Jerome replied.

"You lie!" Christ told him, and the words hit him like a hammer. "You are a Ciceronian, not a Christian."[3]

When he woke from his vision, Jerome swore off classical literature forever. But he couldn't swear off its effect on him. He had absorbed Cicero's style so thoroughly that it had become his natural way of speaking. And everyone who met him, and almost inevitably argued with him about something, had to agree that Jerome certainly knew all the tricks of rhetoric.

Jerome was a famously prickly character. It's probably better for us that we have sixteen centuries between us and him. The people who had to endure Jerome in life praised his talents, but some of them avoided his presence.

"A certain Jerome, a priest, who used to live in these parts, distinguished Latin writer and cultivated scholar as he was, showed qualities of temper so disastrous that they threw into the shade his splendid achievements." That was how Palladius remembered Jerome. He continued, "Posidonius, who had lived with him many days, said in my ear, 'The noble Paula, who looks after him, will die first and be freed from his bad temper. That's what I think. And because of this man no holy man will dwell in these parts, but his envy will include even his own brother.'" Palladius goes on to list a number of talented monks who had been driven away by Jerome's forceful personality.[4]

But others were drawn to him. Those splendid achievements Palladius mentioned were really splendid. Jerome knew Latin and Greek, and he learned Hebrew from Jewish teachers so that he could read the Old Testament in the original.

And perhaps he was a different man when his students were women. One of the remarkable things about Jerome was that a group of extraordinarily talented women coalesced around him.

Of course, people talked. "It often happened that I found myself surrounded with virgins, and to some of these I often expounded the divine books as best I could. Our studies kept us together constantly, which soon ripened into intimacy, and this in turn produced mutual confidence." But no one could accuse him of anything improper. "If they have ever seen anything in my conduct unbecoming a Christian, let them say so. . . . Has my language been equivocal, or my eye wanton? . . . Did I ever cross the threshold of any fast female? Was I ever fascinated by silk dresses, or sparkling jewels, or a made-up face, or a display of gold?"[5]

Jerome thought it was because of these nasty rumors that he was never made pope (although, remembering the opinion of Palladius, we might imagine another explanation). But the rumors were just that—rumors. No one who investigated the matter ever found anything improper going on. And probably the best indication that nothing but intellectual discussion was occurring was how much both Jerome and the women around him learned from these conversations. Jerome's female disciples became some of the leading intellectual lights of Rome—something that had been almost unheard of before then. Female intellectuals? It hardly made sense. But, again, those Christians were marked by the notion that "there is neither male nor female; for you are all one in Christ Jesus" (Gal 3:28).

Paula, who "looked after him" (and perhaps did wear herself out doing it, since—as Posidonius had predicted—she died early, well before Jerome), was one of those intellectual women. And perhaps the most accomplished of them all was Marcella.

Marcella was a noble Roman lady who had decided to live as a nun. It was something that was just not done in those days, as Jerome remembered. "In that time none of the noble women at Rome had been acquainted with the monastic profession; it was thought ignominious and vile among the people to assume the name of monk."[6] But Marcella had met the great Athanasius, who told her all about the life of his teacher Anthony, the founder of monasticism in the Egyptian desert, and about the large communities founded by Pachomius. So Marcella decided she would found an institution like that in Rome.

And then came Jerome. His reputation had preceded him, and Marcella had a voracious curiosity to learn as much as she could about the scriptures. "She never came to me without asking me something about the Scriptures. Nor would she acquiesce immediately, but on the contrary she would bring up questions—not to dispute, but so that by questioning she could get to know the solutions if anyone argued against them."[7]

She became so well versed in the scriptures that, after Jerome left Rome, people in the Church would come to Marcella with any questions they had about the scriptures and Christian doctrine. Jerome gives Marcella credit for settling the controversy that erupted over the works of Origen, the already-ancient Christian writer, whose works apparently were being circulated with some heretical additions and emendations.

His skill as a rhetorician, and his success as a teacher, would have been enough to make Jerome one of the leading intellectual figures of his age. But his greatest achievement, the one we remember him for today, would be as a translator.

Up Close and Personal:

ST. MONICA OF HIPPO

Like most women in the remote African provinces, Monica probably had no opportunities for education. She could read enough, perhaps, to understand the signs in the marketplace. She married young; and her husband, Patrick, was rough around the edges and decidedly not Christian.

Hers was an unpromising path to fame and influence. Yet she is alive in the telling of history today—and for many reasons.

Christians remember Monica as a model of persevering prayer. For seventeen years she begged God to give her stubborn son Augustine the grace of conversion. Augustine, meanwhile, rebuffed her efforts repeatedly. He even lied to her so that she'd lose his trail and stop following him. Riding the wave of his brilliant career, he went to Rome and then to the imperial court in Milan. He seemed unstoppable. The most brilliant intellectual alive, he was dismissive of the arguments of the experts his mother trotted out to persuade him.

Nevertheless, she persisted, and she prevailed—or God did. Augustine, in his dialogues, refers to his illiterate mother as his master in philosophy. His description of her final days is perhaps the single most famous passage in the literature of late antiquity.

Monica's son went on to become one of the most influential figures in all of human history. But he always gave credit to his mother. She deserves it.

The Vulgate

To Jerome, the scriptures were the source of all wisdom. But very few people in the West knew Greek anymore—the language of the New Testament. And almost nobody knew Hebrew, the language of the Old Testament.

There were Latin translations of the books of the Bible. But they weren't very accurate. What was needed was a completely accurate translation in the language of the *vulgus*—the common people—which was Latin.

Jerome was just the man to do it, Pope Damasus thought. So he asked Jerome to undertake the work, and Jerome couldn't refuse. "The labor is one of love, but at the same time both perilous and presumptuous," he wrote to Damasus. It was easy to imagine how people who were attached to the old translations might "call me a forger and a profane man for having the audacity to add anything to the ancient books, or to make any changes in them." But, on the other hand, "the command is given by you who are the supreme bishop."[8]

Bible translations are usually the work of a large committee. The Greek translation of the Old Testament that the earliest Christians used was known as the Septuagint, because it was said to have been the work of a committee of seventy translators. Almost any English version of the Bible you pick up today is the product of a committee just as large.

But Jerome was going to tackle the whole Bible pretty much on his own.

And he would have to start by figuring out what the Bible was.

Surprisingly, in all the great debates over doctrine, the question of which books counted as scripture didn't come up. There had been fringe sects, like the Gnostics, who had their own bizarre scriptures. But in the mainstream of Christianity, there wasn't much debate. The Arian side and the Catholic side had different interpretations of scripture, but they were arguing about the same books.

The Old Testament was inherited from the Jewish tradition, although Christians accepted all the books in the Septuagint, whereas the main body of Judaism had later rejected some of the more recent of the ancient books. Jerome, taught Old Testament Hebrew by rabbis, had his own doubts about the authority of those books; but he translated them anyway, and the Catholic Church accepts them as scripture. (These are the books we call "deuterocanonical." Today, most Protestants reject them, but Catholic and Orthodox Christians accept them as equal in authority to the rest of the Old Testament.)

The New Testament is a more interesting case. The canon—the list of books that can be read in the liturgy, which is what it means to be scripture—just sort of came together. Surprisingly, there had really been no official decree of the Church on the New Testament canon until a year before Jerome published his translation of the four gospels. And even that wasn't a meeting of the whole Church, but only a local council in Rome.

Yet there had been almost unanimous agreement about almost all the books from very early times—probably from early enough that there were still people alive who remembered seeing the apostles and evangelists write those books.

The earliest complete listing of the New Testament is a scrap of vellum called the Muratorian Canon. It was a very exciting thing when it was discovered. And the most exciting thing about it was how unexciting it was. Here was a listing of the New Testament books from the 100s (scholars commonly date it to about 170) that was almost identical to the table of contents in our New Testament today. There are four gospels (we know that there were only four accepted gospels at a much earlier date even than this), the Acts of the Apostles, all the letters of Paul that we know, and the book of Revelation. Minor differences occur in some of the short letters by other apostles: Jude is mentioned, but only two letters (not three) of John; James is not mentioned, and the letters of Peter are also left out—probably. The Latin is very ungrammatical and obscure; the only copy we have was made in the 600s, the depths of the "Dark Ages," and it is possible that some text has dropped out. As it stands, the text says that "we receive the apocalypses of John and Peter only, but some of us do not wish that of Peter to be read in church." If some text has been lost, the original reading might have been something about the apocalypse of John and the two letters of Peter. But there is an "Apocalypse of Peter" that circulated among the Christians in early times. The document's biggest surprise is that it mentions the Wisdom of Solomon with the New Testament; today we put it in the Old Testament.

Except for a few books open to debate, then, the canon of the New Testament was already agreed on before the year 200. Not long before 382, when Jerome started his translation of the Bible, Athanasius had mentioned the canon in a letter, and by Jerome's time there was really no question about it among Christians. Jerome felt comfortable raising questions about the Old Testament, but there was no need to ask what belonged in the New Testament.

It would take more than two decades for Jerome to finish his translation of the Bible—sometimes by revising the old Latin translations, often translating fresh from the original languages, and always making sure his translation was as literally faithful as he could make it.

The Church still uses the Vulgate as its standard reference version. Modern scholars often turn to it to find the meaning of obscure passages in the Bible. Jerome was such a careful translator, and the manuscripts he had to work with were so much closer to the originals, that his version may sometimes preserve a reading that has been obscured by centuries of transmission since his time. Jerome was a great rhetorician and a great teacher, but his greatest monument of all is the Bible in Latin.

But his contemporaries were undoubtedly right. As great a scholar as he was, he probably would have made a lousy pope.

Africa's Wayward Son

While St. Jerome was busy scribbling his translation of the Bible, Augustine was thinking about becoming a Christian.

We met Augustine, who came from Roman Africa, earlier. His mother, Monica, was a Christian, but his father was a pagan. Although Monica did her best to raise her son as a Christian, Augustine was too intellectual for that stuff. "I didn't feel the way I do now about the Scriptures,"

Augustine recalled later. "They seemed undignified to me when I compared them to Cicero's stately eloquence. My swelling pride pulled away from their lowliness, and my sharp wit couldn't penetrate to the depths of them. The Scriptures were the sort of thing that would grow up with little ones. But I scorned to be little. Puffed up with pride, I thought I was something great."[9]

There was a group that attracted him, though. The Manichees had a theology that used big words and long sentences. They certainly *sounded* intellectual. The Manichees rejected the Old Testament, and they believed that the world had been made by an evil creator. Thus, matter was evil; the world was divided between good and evil principles, and the ultimate goal was for the good soul to escape the evil body. All this was expressed in prose that was hard to understand, which made it much more suitable for a proud Ciceronian.

Augustine, like Jerome, studied classical rhetoric, and he was good enough to become a much-in-demand teacher of the art. He lived a life of general intellectual ease; he had a mistress he was rather fond of, though he never married her, and they had a son together. His poor mother prayed a great deal for him, but her prayers never seemed to be answered. Augustine just grew more and more worldly. He even drifted away from the Manichees.

Much against his mother's wishes, the ambitious Augustine left Africa to seek fame and fortune as a rhetoric teacher. He ended up in Milan—and there he came in contact with Ambrose. Ambrose was different from his stereotype of the simple and ignorant Christian. He was obviously a man with a towering intellect, and—as Augustine could appreciate better than anybody—a master of rhetoric. But he was also a firm Catholic Christian, and he could express *why* he was a Christian clearly and beautifully.

More and more, Augustine was beginning to think his mother had been right all along. But he still couldn't quite bring himself to accept Christianity completely.

Then one day, as he was torturing himself in miserable indecision, Augustine heard a child's voice singing in the house next door: "Take it, read it, take it, read it . . ."

It sounded like some nursery rhyme, but Augustine had never heard a nursery rhyme like it before. Was it a message from God?

There was a copy of St. Paul's letter to the Romans on the table in the next room. Augustine dashed in, picked it up, and read the first thing his eyes fell on: "not in reveling and drunkenness, not in debauchery and licentiousness, not in quarreling and jealousy. But put on the Lord Jesus Christ, and make no provision for the flesh, to gratify its desires" (Rom 13:13–14).

From that moment, Augustine was a Christian. He had himself baptized—along with his teenage son—by the great Ambrose in Milan.

A Revolution in Introspection

Augustine ended up back in Africa, ultimately as bishop of Hippo, a city not far from Carthage. He applied all his knowledge of classical philosophy to Christian theology, creating an enormous body of carefully reasoned writing that it would be safe to say has never been surpassed, and only rarely equaled.

But Augustine's greatest contribution to world literature isn't a work of deep theology—or at least it's only incidentally a work of deep theology. We know so much about Augustine's long road to Christianity because Augustine invented the genre of autobiography.

Of course, Augustine wasn't the first person to write about his own life. Famous men had always recorded their great achievements. Julius Caesar wrote an account of his conquest of Gaul that became one of the great classics of Latin literature. And we have an earlier example in the Bible, where much of the book of Nehemiah is made up of Nehemiah's own memoirs.

But no one before Augustine had made such a thorough search of his own soul. Everything we think of as essential to autobiography today—the minute chronicling of thoughts, feelings, and impressions, the relentless self-examination—comes from St. Augustine's *Confessions*. It's one of the two books by Augustine that can claim a place among the foremost works of world literature.

The other book would come later. It would have to wait for the end of the world.

Chapter 10

Decline and Fall

The emperor must be told. Through the arcades of the palace in Ravenna the messenger ran, past rows of priceless statues, past imaginary landscapes so skillfully painted they looked like windows, through the great audience chamber, between the clucking chickens, and—much out of breath—into the presence of the august emperor Honorius himself.

There was no breath left for formalities. "Rome has perished!" the messenger cried.

The emperor looked up in horror from the fancy chickens he had been feeding and clucking over.

"What? But she was just eating out of my hand an hour ago!"

The messenger stared blankly. He breathed heavily for a few moments, and then tried again.

"Alaric has conquered Rome. The Goths are sacking the city even now."

"Oh," the emperor said. And then he broke into a happy laugh. "Oh! I thought you meant my *chicken* named Rome! But look—she's fine. There she is now. Come here, Rome, sweetie. Cluck cluck! I have a treat for you! Cluck cluck!"

He couldn't yet take it in.

Conquered Is the Conqueror

"While this is going on in Jebus," Jerome wrote, "a terrible rumor is brought in from the West: Rome besieged, the safety of her citizens ransomed with gold; plundered, they are surrounded again, so that after their possessions they lose their lives. My voice catches, and sobs cut off the words I'm dictating. Conquered is the city that conquered the whole world! She was wasted by the most profound famine before the sword, and it was hard to find any left to be captured. A frenzy of hunger burst forth in abominable food, and they tore at each other's limbs, while the mother did not spare her suckling infant, and took back in her belly what a little while before she had discharged from it."[1]

Jerome is probably exaggerating here. Accomplished rhetorician that he is, he gives us a catalog of horrors we might expect in the story of a besieged and sacked city.

But there's no mistaking the real feeling in his words. Jerome was in the Holy Land when he heard the news that Rome had fallen ("Jebus" is his poetical Old Testament name for Jerusalem), and it felt like the end of the world. Rome *couldn't* be sacked. The whole world depended on it. True, the actual capitals of the Empire were Constantinople and now Ravenna, but Rome was . . . Rome. It stood for the order of the universe.

How did it come to this? How did the city of Rome, untouched by foreign invaders for eight hundred years, fall prey to the Goths, while the useless emperor sat in Ravenna and tended his fancy poultry?

It started with Theodosius the Great.

Autumn of the Empire

After the battle of Adrianople, Theodosius had been left to mop up the mess. He did a spectacularly good job of it, too, considering how little he had to work with.

The Goths were a Germanic tribe who had been converted to Arian Christianity by Ulfilas, as you'll remember. They were pushing westward into Roman territory, probably because they were being pushed in the east by the Huns. Valens had invited some of them to settle in the depopulated frontier provinces; when too many showed up, the result was famine, which the Roman government did nothing to alleviate. The Goths rebelled and won the battle of Adrianople.

Four years later they signed a peace treaty, after it had become obvious that Theodosius was enough of a general to keep the Goths from making any progress. Theodosius gave them very good terms: they were basically given an autonomous state within Roman borders (the Romans had abandoned that frontier land anyway, because it was constantly being overrun by Goths) in return for serving under Gothic generals in the Roman army.

It was a delicate balancing act. Theodosius was counting on barbarians to defend Rome's frontiers from barbarians. He was betting he could keep them in control with an elaborate system of carrots and sticks.

And it worked very well as long as Theodosius was in charge. Things seemed to get back to normal. The Roman Empire was a bit beat up but intact, and you could travel once again from one end to the other without worrying too much about violence along the way.

In fact, it was once again a good time to be a tourist.

Pilgrimages to the Holy Land were popular and safe in the Christian Empire. We get a vivid picture of one of these pilgrimages from a woman named Egeria, who visited the Holy Land in about 384. She saw the Church of the Nativity in Bethlehem and all the holy sites in Jerusalem, which had been adorned with churches to receive the crowds of pilgrims.

It seemed that Christianity and the Empire were both in a healthy state. A woman could undertake a trip to Palestine and write about it—an indication of how much the status of women had changed since pagan times, and an indication of how secure people felt under Theodosius the Great. His policy of settling barbarians in vacant Roman territory was working; the barbarians formed a defensive buffer on the borders, and the wastelands were growing productive again. As long as Theodosius was in charge, it all worked smoothly.

And then, quite unexpectedly, Theodosius died in 395.

He left the Empire to his two sons: Arcadius in the East and Honorius in the West. And it quickly became clear that the one thing Theodosius had been no good at was raising children.

Arcadius, who was sixteen years old when he took over, was useless. Honorius, who was ten, was worse than useless. He was a little boy when he became absolute ruler of the West, and he never really grew up. Twenty-eight years later, when he faded out of existence, he was still mentally a child. He's the one we found playing among the chickens at the opening of this chapter.

Of course, there could be no question of Honorius leading the armies himself. So the power passed into the hands of a half-Roman, half-Vandal general named Stilicho. (The Vandals were another Germanic tribe that Theodosius had dealt with.)

With Theodosius gone, every barbarian tribe seemed to decide at once to see how far it could push into the heart of the Empire. To keep the figurehead Honorius safe as battles raged in Italy itself, Stilicho suggested that Honorius move his capital from Milan, which was always near the fighting, to Ravenna, an easily defended city on the coast that was out of the way of the main targets. So Honorius spent the rest of his life in Ravenna concentrating on the one thing that really interested him, which was fancy poultry.

Stilicho was a talented general who managed to keep the Goths at bay until the year 408. In that year, Honorius displayed his one other character trait besides poultry fancying: vicious ingratitude. Goaded by envious courtiers, he had Stilicho executed, along with all his most experienced officers. And with no Stilicho to stand in their way, Alaric and his Gothic horde walked right down to Rome and besieged the city. Alaric waited for Honorius to offer him terms of peace. But Honorius, who had a spectacular genius for the wrong thing at the wrong time, refused to negotiate—as if he even had anything to negotiate with. So Alaric sacked Rome and left with everything portable.

Why did Rome fall?

One answer was that Honorius was an incompetent dolt.

But for people at that time, the question needed more of an answer. It had been eight hundred years since Rome had been invaded by a foreign enemy. Something was wrong with the universe.

There were still a good number of pagans among Rome's conservative upper class, and they argued that the answer was simple: the Christians were to blame. The ancient gods had always protected Rome; but now they were no longer worshiped properly, and they were angry.

Refugees poured out of Rome across the sea to Africa—especially members of the upper class who could afford to make the trip. Augustine heard their arguments about the Christians being responsible for the fall of Rome, and he felt he owed the world a response. So he started writing.

He might have started out to write a pamphlet, but the more he thought about the subject, the more there was to think about. He ended up writing his longest and most elaborate work, and his most famous after the *Confessions*: a massive book called *The City of God*.

Augustine pointed out that, in spite of the looting and violence, the sack of Rome had been very different from other defeats of great cities in the past. The Goths were Christians, and "what was new," Augustine wrote, "was that savage barbarians showed themselves in so gentle a guise that the largest churches were chosen and set aside to be filled with people to whom quarter was given, where none were killed, and from which none were dragged by force. Many were led by their relenting enemies to be set free, and from them none were led into slavery by merciless foes. Whoever does not see that this is to be attributed to the name of Christ and to his era is blind."[2]

Jerome, by the way, confirms what Augustine said about the places of refuge. His friend Marcella was beaten by Gothic soldiers when she insisted that she had no possessions to loot. But other Goths rescued her and took her to the basilica of St. Paul, one of the places of refuge Augustine mentioned.[3] Marcella died a few days later, possibly from her injuries. The Gothic soldiers were not kind and gentle. But the idea of places of refuge for citizens while the soldiers looted was something new in war.

Augustine went on to his main point, which he developed for the rest of the book. There are two cities: the earthly city and the city of God. The two cities are mixed up together in this world, but Christians belong to the city of God. And we know that our citizenship is eternal, whereas the earthly city must pass away by nature.

And the earthly city did seem to be passing away. Especially in the West, the Empire seemed to be flying to bits.

Up in Britain, Saxons—more Germanic tribes—were pushing in from the sea to the east. Most of the Roman soldiers had been pulled out to defend Italy, and the British were left without any defense. The once-prosperous province was collapsing in chaos. Desperate Britons sent a plea to the emperor for help. Unfortunately, the emperor was Honorius and the year was 410, the year of the Gothic sack of Rome. Honorius graciously gave the British permission to solve the problem themselves. And that is why we speak a Germanic language, not a Celtic or Romance language.

In spite of all these shocks, the Church still found time for more controversies. The two biggest controversies neatly divided themselves between West and East.

In the West, specifically from Roman Britain, there was a moralist named Pelagius who began to stir up a mess when he got into an argument with Augustine about free will. Pelagius believed that it was possible for a human being to merit salvation on his own, without divine help. We could live without sin by our own will and effort. Augustine, on the other hand, believed that we could avoid sin only with God's grace. The "Pelagians" became particularly strong in Britain, where you might have thought the Saxons would be in enough trouble without adding theological controversies.

Pope Innocent I decided against the Pelagians in 417, but of course that didn't make the controversy go away. Part of Augustine's busy intellectual life was devoted to writing tracts against the Pelagians. And, believe it or not, he still had Donatists to deal with. It had been one hundred years since the Donatists broke away from the Catholic Church (or, from the Donatist point of view, since the entire Church apostasized except for the small Donatist remnant) because they couldn't accept penitent *traditores*. Now the Donatists were a separate, parallel church that had somehow gotten itself mixed up with dangerous antigovernment terrorists.

In the East, a much bigger storm was brewing.

Up Close and Personal:

PILGRIMS OF THE FOURTH CENTURY

Travel in the ancient world wasn't exactly easy. Nonetheless, many Christians undertook long pilgrimages. Two of the most famous Christian pilgrims were women. Helena, the mother of the Emperor Constantine, brought several holy relics (with various degrees of authenticity) back with her to Rome in the late 320s. A pilgrim from the Western Roman Empire named Egeria wrote a diary of her travels to Christian sites in the Middle East in the 380s. Parts of her detailed narrative can still be read. Favorite pilgrim sites included:

1. The Holy Land, especially the sites related to Jesus
2. Rome, especially the tombs of Sts. Peter and Paul
3. Mount Sinai, Egypt, where Moses received the Law; site of Christian monasteries
4. Abu Mena (near Alexandria, Egypt), the burial site of St. Menas, a soldier who died a martyr under Diocletian
5. Shrine of St. Babylas the Martyr, near Syrian Antioch

Nestorius and the Mother of God

The new bishop of Constantinople was a man named Nestorius, whom some thought was less than qualified for the second-most-important position in the Church. "Having read through the writings of Nestorius myself," wrote the historian Socrates, "I have found him an uneducated man."[4]

Socrates tells us how the controversy started. Nestorius had brought a priest named Anastasius with him from Antioch, and it was Anastasius who dropped the first bombshell. Preaching in church one day, he said, "Let no one call Mary 'Mother of God': for Mary was a mere human being, and it is impossible that God should be born of a human being."

"This caused a great sensation," Socrates tells us, "and troubled both the clergy and the laity, as they had been taught up to now to acknowledge Christ as God, and by no means to separate his humanity from his divinity on account of the economy of salvation." The title "Mother of God," moreover, had been commonplace in the Church's devotion for centuries. The Marian prayer known as the *Sub Tuum Praesidium* ("We fly to your patronage . . .") exists in manuscripts dating back to the third century, and it addresses Mary as "Mother of God." Julian the Apostate mocked Christians for their constant and, as he saw it, illogical invocation of Mary as the forebear of eternal God.

Nevertheless, Nestorius supported his old friend Anastasius, and he dug in. He completely rejected the term "Mother of God"—in Greek, *Theotokos*. "He seemed afraid of the word *Theotokos*, as if it were some terrible phantom," Socrates wrote. "In fact, the baseless fear he showed on this subject merely exposed his extreme ignorance. For he was a naturally fluent speaker, so he was considered well educated; but actually he was disgracefully illiterate."[5]

In a way, Nestorianism, as this new idea came to be called, was just an extreme reaction against Arianism. It was the pendulum swinging too far in the other direction. The Arians denied that Christ was true God. The Nestorians placed so much emphasis on his divinity that they couldn't bear to see it mixed up with mere humanity.

Once again, a new idea was being preached in the church in Constantinople. And once again, its chief opponent was the bishop of Alexandria.

Cyril vs. Nestorius

Cyril of Alexandria is one of those prickly characters in history. Like Jerome, he made great contributions to Christian theology, but you wouldn't want to negotiate a settlement with him.

We might as well deal with the biggest stain on Cyril's reputation right away. Alexandria was the intellectual heart of the Roman Empire, and in the early 400s the brightest intellectual light in Alexandria was Hypatia. She was a pagan and a philosopher, and—uniquely in the history of pagan philosophy—she was a woman. She had many friends among the Christian intellectuals, some of whom regarded her as their greatest teacher.

In 415, Cyril the bishop was having trouble with the governor Orestes, and a false rumor went around that Hypatia had poisoned Orestes's mind against Cyril. Alexandria, as we have seen, was a city often on the edge of a riot, and this rumor was enough to set one off. A mob of Cyril's supporters ambushed Hypatia, murdered her gruesomely, and dismembered her body.

We know about this dreadful business because the Christian historian Socrates was horrified by it. "This affair brought no small opprobrium, not only on Cyril, but also on the whole Alexandrian church. And surely nothing can be further from the spirit of Christians than massacres and fights and such."[6]

Although Cyril himself may not have had anything to do with it, the murder of such a precious treasure as Hypatia was hard to forgive. And Cyril's well-known temper made him, unfairly perhaps, suspected of complicity in her murder.

With all we hear from the writers of the time about how hard Cyril was to get along with, we're almost surprised to see that his early correspondence with Nestorius seems measured and polite. It's important, Cyril wrote, to be careful when we explain doctrine to the people, and you seem to be dividing the Lord Jesus Christ into two sons. That goes against the true doctrine of the holy Fathers, who always boldly called Mary "Mother of God" because the Word himself became flesh. *I beg you as a brother*, he said, to teach the same things the rest of the Church teaches.[7]

Nestorius responded by objecting to the insulting tone of Cyril's letter, which suggests that Nestorius himself was even more prickly than Cyril.

Both Cyril and Nestorius sent letters to Pope Celestine in Rome. The pope decided in favor of Cyril, and then took an extraordinary step: he granted Cyril all the authority of the Roman see in dealing with Nestorius. Anything Cyril said, anything he did, would have the power of the pope in Rome behind it.[8]

Armed with that power, Cyril dealt straightforwardly with Nestorius—high-handedly, some said at the time. Here's what you have to teach, he said. If you don't, you're no longer a bishop. Cyril gave Nestorius a list of twelve points he had to reject. We have been taught the true faith by the apostles, the evangelists, the scriptures, and the Fathers of the Church, Cyril wrote, and that is the faith you must teach.[9]

Nestorius didn't want to take that from Cyril, of course. He and his supporters accused Cyril of Arianism. A council was called at Ephesus, where Cyril triumphed—although he didn't quite give Nestorius's supporters time to get there. (To be fair, it wouldn't have made a difference. Cyril had overwhelming numbers on his side.)

The Council of Ephesus's biggest innovation was a kind of anti-innovation. For the first time, a council of bishops decided that the Nicene Creed was the permanent standard, and no revised or substitute creed should ever be composed.

Nestorius was furious, and he blamed it all on Cyril. "Who was judge? Cyril! Who was accuser? Cyril! Who was bishop of Rome? Cyril! Cyril was everything!"[10]

Nestorius was exiled. His legacy continued, however, in the Church of the East, which even today venerates him as a saint. After a millennium and a half, this "Nestorian" body began a process of reconciliation with the Catholic Church under Pope John Paul II, who approved intercommunion with its members under certain circumstances.

The ending of any chapter in history is an arbitrary point. Even the ancient stories continue long after they seem to be concluded. Nevertheless, we turn to a final chapter in our account.

YOU BE THE JUDGE:

Isn't the Church's Marian piety a fifth-century innovation?

"All generations will call me blessed," Mary predicted (Lk 1:48), and that was no exaggeration. Through the early centuries of Christian history, Marian devotion was constant in the Church's life.

Mary's role in the gospels is undeniable. In Matthew, the Gentiles encounter their Savior through her mediation (Mt 2:11). In Luke, she plays the most important role in the first two chapters, one of the largest speaking parts in the New Testament, and she appears to be one of the author's most important sources of information. In John, she manages to advance the hour of Jesus' public ministry (Jn 2:3–7), and at the Cross she is named as the mother of Jesus' beloved disciple (Jn 19:26–27). St. Paul, in his briefest summary of salvation history, skips over most of the details, but needs to mention her (Gal 4:4). In Revelation, she appears in heaven as the mother of the Messiah (Rv 12:1f).

The generation afterward reflected on Mary's role as they preached the Gospel. St. Ignatius of Antioch, writing in AD 107, makes mention of her. And in the early apocrypha—the *Ascension of Isaiah* and the *Protoevangelium of James*, for example—she plays a central role.

The Marian prayer known as the *Sub Tuum Praesidium* enters the documentary record in the third century, but was probably already traditional by then: "We fly to your patronage, O holy Mother of God: despise not our petitions in our necessities, but deliver us from all danger, O ever glorious and blessed Virgin Mary!"

Mary is crucial in the theology of the early Fathers, especially St. Irenaeus and Origen. Her image is everywhere: in the Roman catacombs and in the cemeteries of the Fayoum in Egypt. Apparitions of her were reported in every one of the first six centuries. The persecutor Julian mocked believers for their incessant invocation of the Mother of God.

The Council of Ephesus in 431 drew from these historic riches as the bishops responded to the heresy of Nestorius, who denied Mary the title of "Mother of God." But the Council of Ephesus presented no innovations. It simply affirmed the long-standing Christian tradition of calling upon Mary as the mother Jesus gave to the Church as he suffered on the Cross.

Chapter 11

A Lamp in the Twilight

It's a sight to make your heart stop and your knees turn to jelly. As far as the eye can see, Huns. Tents full of Huns, fields of Huns, Huns on horses, Huns on foot, Huns laughing, Huns cooking, Huns drinking. From here to the horizon, not a single Hun-free square foot of ground.

And in the near distance, several thousand Hunnish faces scrutinizing their well-dressed Roman visitors—some with curiosity, some with amusement, some with obvious contempt. It is only forty-two years since Alaric and his Goths stormed the city. It is keen in Rome's collective memory, and so is the awareness that this present enemy is far more dangerous.

Right in the middle of the Huns stands a big tent, a tent like a palace, dripping with precious hangings and weavings.

"He's been in there a while," says the consul.

"Yes," the praetorian prefect agrees.

They gaze at the tent a little longer.

"I mean a good *long* while," the consul adds.

"If you want to go in there and rescue him, I won't stop you," the praetorian prefect says.

They both look over the thousand or so Huns between them and the big tent.

"We can wait," the consul says, and the praetorian prefect nods in agreement.

And then they see movement down at the tent. A figure in white robes trimmed with purple and embroidered in gold emerges, flanked by Hunnish soldiers. The other two Romans watch as the Huns part respectfully to make way for Attila's guest. He approaches slowly; it seems to take forever. But at last he is facing them.

"Attila has agreed," the pope tells his Roman companions.

"Agreed?" the consul asks. He wasn't expecting any good news at all, and his mind is having trouble adjusting to it. "Agreed to what?"

"To turn back," the pope says. "Attila will leave Italy and go back across the Danube. Rome will not be attacked."

The other two Romans look at each other. They look back at Pope Leo. This is impossibly good news.

"But, your Holiness. . . . What did you say?" the consul asks at last.

"Oh, I . . . explained to him that it might be best."

The Empire Vanishes

What did Leo the Great say to Attila the Hun?

It's one of history's great unanswered questions. We know that Attila and his numberless horde of Huns were on their way down the Italian peninsula toward Rome. We know that the Romans had no way of stopping them. And we know that, after meeting with the pope, Attila promised peace, turned around, and retreated back across the Danube.

Why?

Some historians think Attila might have had his own reasons. He might have been running out of supplies, with no prospect of more. His army might have been stretched to the limit in already-ravaged Italy. Others suspect Leo might have played on Attila's well-known superstition. Remember Alaric? he might have said. Alaric sacked Rome, and shortly after that he was dead.

The one thing we do know is that Rome had run out of options. The only leader Rome could rely on was her bishop, who was forced to take on the role of the government because there was no longer an effective government.

The Western Empire had fallen apart. Britain was gone, with the Roman British fighting each other as much as the Saxons. Large parts of Gaul were gone. Spain was gone. All that was left of the Roman Empire in western Europe was Italy and a few adjacent areas. And barbarian hordes were constantly penetrating even Italy.

Most catastrophic of all, Africa was gone—Africa, the breadbasket of Italy. Where would Italy get her grain with Africa in barbarian hands?

Aside from the Huns—no one really knows where the Huns came from—most of these invaders were Germanic tribes: Saxons, Franks, Goths, Vandals.

It was the Vandals who took Africa. The fall of Africa actually began, however, with internal terrorists: local tribes aided and abetted by the Donatist bandits who seemed to huddle around the tombs until there was an opportunity for another lightning raid. As Africa destabilized, the Vandals who had occupied Spain saw an opportunity.

In 429, the Vandals arrived. In 430, they besieged Hippo at the northern tip of Africa. Probably many of the people who found themselves trapped were refugees who had fled after the sack of Rome to find a haven on the more peaceful continent to the south.

The aging Augustine of Hippo, now in his middle seventies, refused to leave his flock even as the Vandals approached. In a time when government had fallen apart, the bishop was the only one the people could rely on. "Whoever flees from danger when his flight does not deprive the Church of the service it needs is doing what the Lord commanded or permitted," he explained. "But the minister who flees when his flight takes away from Christ's flock the nourishment that sustains its spiritual life—that minister is a hireling who sees the wolf coming and flees because he does not care for the sheep."[1]

As their world collapsed around them, again the Romans asked, *Why?*

And there were some who dared to answer, *because we deserve it.*

"But as for the way the Goths and Vandals live—how can we think we're better than they are in any way, or even comparable?" So wrote Salvian, who lived in Gaul as it was passing from Roman to barbarian hands. "First, there's their love and charity. . . . Almost all the barbarians (or at least the ones who belong to a single tribe under a single king) love one another. But almost all the Romans are at each other's throats. Who among the citizens doesn't envy the others? Who really has charity for his neighbors? . . . It's not enough for anyone to be happy himself. No, someone else has to be made miserable."[2]

Salvian's argument was that the barbarians were morally superior to the Romans, and the Empire was falling apart because of the sins of the people.

Regardless of the reason, it was clear that the old order was giving way to the new. And it was equally clear that civilization itself was fading all across the West.

Still, there were lamps being lit here and there, sometimes in the remotest corners.

Lights in the Darkness

Monasteries were flourishing even as the rest of the West was collapsing. Christian barbarians usually left them alone, and they kept the flame of learning alive when no one else had time to tend it.

Martin of Tours was one of the early planters of monasticism in the West. He had a thriving monastery by the late 300s, though it was a much smaller institution than the giant Eastern monasteries that made new cities in the desert. But one fact in particular stands out in the description of Martin's community by his biographer Sulpicius Severus: "No trade was practiced there except that of the copyist."[3]

Copying books, then, had already become an essentially monkish activity. It was probably practiced in the time of Martin because copying books was a good way for the monks to learn from them. Books weren't rare yet; even a century later, in the late 400s, Sidonius Apollinaris wrote of bookstores lined with books as common sights in post-Roman Gaul. But as the darkness descended, monasteries would be ready to do the work of preserving Western literature.

Meanwhile, as the Roman Empire was contracting, Christendom was expanding.

The story of St. Patrick reminds us how perilous life could be as Roman power disintegrated—and how often Christians responded heroically to the perils.

Patrick came from a Christian British family; he was the son of a deacon who was the son of a priest. (In those days, married clergy were common.) But Patrick tells us that as a young man he didn't know God; perhaps he means that he was not an enthusiastic Christian.

When Patrick was sixteen, heathen raiders from Ireland descended on his part of Britain and took him away as a slave, along with thousands of others. While Patrick was kept in Ireland working as a herdsman, he had a conversion experience and began to pray fervently and frequently every day. His prayers were answered: after six years in slavery, he escaped back to his family in Britain.

After several uneventful years, he had a dream in which a man came to him bearing a huge number of letters. Patrick took one and read it. It was headed *The Voice of the Irish*, and it begged him to come back to Ireland, which was the last place Patrick wanted to go. In fact, he seems to have resisted the idea for years. But he did eventually return to the Irish—as their bishop. And no one in the English- or Irish-speaking world has to be told how grateful the Irish are for that.

Up Close and Personal:
IRISH CATHOLICS

St. Patrick is usually credited with evangelizing the people of Ireland, but he wasn't the first to try—or succeed. In 431, a man named Palladius was sent to Ireland by the pope to minister to those who already believed in Christ. Palladius, not Patrick, was Ireland's first bishop. But obviously, he was not the first Christian missionary to set foot on Irish soil. Information about how Christianity came to Ireland is cloudy and uncertain. One thing, however, is sure: when Patrick arrived in the northern part of the island in 432, he won many converts and became popular enough to earn the title of Ireland's patron saint.

It is thought that one of the converts Patrick baptized was a slave woman who gave birth to a daughter named Brigid. By all accounts, Brigid was a pious child. She later became a nun and founded monasteries for both women and men. Known for her great compassion and charity, St. Brigid contributed to the spread of the faith in her homeland. Although she—and not Patrick—envisioned heaven as having a lake of ale, her February 1 feast day has yet to be celebrated with green beer.

Eastern Debates and Byzantine Maneuvers

Meanwhile, as the West was collapsing, the East was still relatively prosperous. The emperor Theodosius II continued his grandfather Theodosius the Great's policy of Catholicizing the Empire. During his reign of more than forty years, pagans were prohibited from serving in the army or government. But he did specifically decree that there was to be no punishment for being a pagan. Pagans who obeyed the laws were not to be bothered.

As the population became more and more thoroughly Christian, a fad for extreme asceticism took hold. Some of these holy men (and sometimes women) practiced holiness as performance art, becoming well-known celebrities. One of the most celebrated was St. Symeon Stylites, who spent many years living on top of a pillar and never coming down. He became a popular tourist attraction, and his example of extreme self-denial probably inspired many ordinary Christians to practice a little more self-denial of their own.

For a few years there seemed to be peace in the Church. The heresies of Arius and Nestorius had forced Catholic theologians to think carefully and deeply about the nature of Christ. It all seemed to be worked out.

Then came Eutyches to show that there was still work to do.

Eutyches was a monk who taught that Christ had only one nature, his divine nature. Taken to its logical extreme, Eutyches's theology implied that Christ was not really human at all. And if he didn't share our nature, what did that mean for our salvation?

Flavian, patriarch of Constantinople, opposed Eutyches. But Eutyches had a powerful ally in the current bishop of Alexandria, Dioscorus. Once again, the whole Eastern Church was in an uproar.

The emperor summoned a council, again at Ephesus. Flavian wrote to Pope Leo in Rome. (This was about three years before Leo's famous meeting with Attila.) Leo responded with a long refutation of Eutyches, a document history remembers as the Tome of Leo. It was a brilliant distillation of Catholic teaching on the nature of Christ. And the council never heard it.

Pope Leo's delegates brought his Tome with them. But when the council convened in early 449, Dioscorus immediately took it over. He announced that Flavian would not be allowed to speak at all, and any bishop who objected would be sent to prison. He declared that Eutyches was Catholic; were there objections from anyone who would like to spend the night in jail? Then he announced that Flavian must be condemned and deposed. He would not allow Leo's letter to be read. When some of the bishops asked for at least a postponement, they found themselves at the pointy ends of swords. And when Flavian appealed to the pope, he was suddenly surrounded by soldiers.

Flavian tried to take refuge at the altar, but the soldiers prevented him. In the brawl, he somehow found his way to a back room in the church, where he barricaded himself in. Dioscorus posted guards to make sure that Flavian didn't get a message out to the pope. But apparently someone had an attack of conscience, because we know about this riotous council—remembered in history by Leo's name for it, the Robber Synod—from the letter Flavian ultimately managed to get out to Leo.

Flavian wasn't exaggerating. We have another account in a letter from Theodoret, bishop of Cyrrhus, who was also deposed by the Robber Synod, and who also wrote to Pope Leo complaining about it.

> For the very righteous bishop of Alexandria was not content with the illegal and very unrighteous deposition of the most holy and godly bishop of Constantinople, the lord Flavian, but he stabbed me with a pen too in my absence, without

summoning me to trial, without questioning me as to my opinions about the incarnation of our God and Savior. Even murderers, tomb-breakers, and adulterers are not condemned by their judges until either they themselves have confirmed the charges against them by confessing them, or have been clearly convicted by the testimony of others. Yet I, nurtured as I have been in the divine laws, have been condemned by him at his pleasure, when all the time I was thirty-five days away.[4]

This high-handed behavior made Dioscorus's predecessor Cyril look like a fluffy kitten by contrast. But his triumph was short-lived. He was sealing his own fate.

Two years later, in 451, another council came together at Chalcedon. This time there would be no ambush, no decisions at sword point. Dioscorus was deposed, and the faith was defined by the standard of Nicaea and Constantinople.

The Council of Chalcedon was the last of the great ecumenical councils on the nature of Christ. The doctrine of the Catholic Church was established as the same in East and West. One faith united the whole Roman Empire.

Or what was left of it.

Believers in the third, fourth, and fifth centuries knew well what Catholics know today: to be a Christian was to obey Jesus Christ in the teaching of his vicar, the pope.

YOU BE THE JUDGE:

Wasn't supreme papal authority an invention of the Middle Ages?

Some people say that papal and Roman primacy was an invention of the Middle Ages. In the very first century, however, St. Clement, the third pope, felt secure enough in his office to write a long letter correcting a congregation in faraway Greece. He urged the Christians of Corinth to "render obedience unto the things written by us through the Holy Spirit." And later he said the words of his letter were "spoken by [Jesus] through us" (St. Clement of Rome, *To the Corinthians*, 59). Those are mighty claims; yet the Corinthians accepted them. A century later, they still read Clement's letter when they gathered for worship.

When the saints of East and West needed support or aid or judgment in practical matters, they appealed to the pope. We find such pleas in the works of St. Irenaeus (second century), St. Cyprian of Carthage (third century), Sts. Athanasius and Basil the Great (fourth century), St. John Chrysostom (early fifth century), St. Cyril of Alexandria (mid-fifth century), and St. Maximus Confessor (sixth century). Sometimes these saints were disappointed by the pope's response, but they maintained their faith in the papal office.

In the year 376, the greatest scripture scholar in the ancient world, Jerome, addressed Pope Damasus I with a litany of biblical symbols of papal authority: "I speak with the successor of the fisherman and disciple of the Cross. Following none but Christ as my primate, I am united in communion with Your Beatitude— that is, with the chair of Peter. Upon that Rock I know the Church is built. Whosoever eats a lamb outside this house is profane. Whoever is not in Noah's ark will perish when the flood prevails" (St. Jerome, *Letters* 15.1).

The End

In 476, the Roman Empire in the West fell.

That's what we always hear. It may be, though, that not many people at the time noticed.

For years, the remains of the Western Empire had been run by generals who appointed figurehead emperors and deposed them when they got ideas. The last of these figureheads was a boy named Romulus; history remembers him as Romulus Augustulus—Romulus the "Little Augustus." In 476, the Gothic general Odoacer, who had overcome the last of the strong Roman generals (Romulus's father, Orestes), decided he could do without the figurehead altogether. Romulus was forced to resign.

A letter from the young emperor, or at least signed by him, was sent to the Eastern emperor Zeno in Constantinople, along with the imperial regalia. It seemed good, the letter said in Romulus's voice, that the Empire should go back to having just one emperor. Romulus's very good friend Odoacer had graciously volunteered to govern Italy in Zeno's name.

So the fiction was maintained that Italy was still part of the Empire. And most of the starving, war-ravaged populace probably didn't think about it too much one way or the other.

The real power of the Empire was gone in the West, and arguably had been gone since Honorius. Western Europe would never again be united in one great empire. Already the map of Europe was beginning to look the way it looks today.

But there was still one force that held the West together. The Catholic Church crossed national boundaries and preserved a culture that was more than tribal.

The long night of what historians used to call the "Dark Ages" was falling. But all over the West, wherever there was a church, wherever there was a monastery, a lamp was burning in the darkness.

Acknowledgments

Thanks to Jon Sweeney for conceiving the idea for this series and inviting me to be general editor.

My main sources for this book are the "ecclesiastical histories" composed in antiquity by Eusebius of Caesarea, Theodoret, Socrates Scholasticus, Sozomen, and Philostorgius. The texts of these works (and others) I have mined from three series of translations produced in the nineteenth century: *A Library of Fathers of the Holy Catholic Church*; *The Ante-Nicene Fathers*; and *The Nicene and Post-Nicene Fathers*. The English language has changed much in the century-and-more since those translations first appeared. I have taken the liberty of modernizing the English to make it accessible to today's readers. Sometimes I have consulted the Latin and Greek originals and produced new translations for the quoted passages.

Two great webmasters have taken up the task of curating and storing these ancient texts in translation: Roger Pearse at Tertullian.org and Kevin Knight at NewAdvent.org. I am deeply grateful to both men for giving me permission to use and adapt their etexts for this book.

Since this book is aimed at a nonacademic audience, I've tried to keep my citations very simple. The original translations can easily be found at the sites mentioned above. I hope many readers will be inspired to pursue the texts and read the original translations in context.

Notes

Chapter 1. The Underground

1. This slightly fictional account is compiled from several historical records, especially *Gesta apud Zenophilum*, in *Corpus Scriptorum Ecclesiasticorum Latinorum*, vol. 26, 186–88.

2. *1 Clement* 44.2.

3. Tacitus, *Annals* 15.44.

4. Suetonius, *Life of Claudius* 25.4.

5. Tacitus, *Annals* 15.44.

6. Tacitus, *Annals* 15.44.

7. Rodney Stark, *The Rise of Christianity: How the Obscure, Marginal Jesus Movement Became the Dominant Religious Force in the Western World in a Few Centuries* (San Francisco: HarperCollins, 1997), 7.

8. Gary B. Ferngren, *Medicine and Health Care in Early Christianity* (Baltimore: Johns Hopkins University Press, 2009), 132.

9. Justin Martyr, *Second Apology* 2.2. Justin's focus is on the martyrs, but he gives quite a detailed account of the married couple who became the occasion of their martyrdom.

10. Tertullian, *Apology* 50.13.

11. Cyprian, *On the Lapsed* 8.

12. Cyprian, *Letters* 55.6.

13. Pontius the Deacon, *Life and Passion of St. Cyprian* 9.

14. St. Dionysius of Alexandria, *Letters* 12, 4.

Chapter 2. The Revolution

1. Eusebius, *Church History* 9.8.

2. Eusebius, *Church History* 9.8.14.

3. Eusebius, *Church History* 9.8.15.

4. Eusebius, *Life of Constantine* 1.28. We have a vivid account of Constantine's vision because Eusebius heard it from Constantine's own lips. There's no telling how much Constantine's memory elaborated the details in later years, but I've used Eusebius as the closest we'll ever get to an eyewitness account.

5. Lactantius, *On the Deaths of the Persecutors* 44.5.

6. Lactantius, *On the Deaths of the Persecutors* 48.

7. Eusebius, *Church History* 10.5.16.

8. Eusebius, *Church History* 10.6.1.

9. Augustine, *Letters* 88.2.

10. Optatus, *On the Schism of the Donatists* 1.22.

11. Eusebius, *Church History* 10.5.18.

12. Letter of Constantine to Aelafius, Vicar of Africa, in J. Stevenson and W. H. C. Frend, *A New Eusebius* (Grand Rapids, MI: Baker, 1987), n. 263.

Chapter 3. Nicaea

1. Socrates, *Ecclesiastical History* 1.5.

2. Socrates, *Ecclesiastical History* 1.5.

3. Sozomen, *Ecclesiastical History* 1.15.

4. Sozomen, *Ecclesiastical History* 1.15.

5. Sozomen, *Ecclesiastical History* 1.15.

6. Sozomen, *Ecclesiastical History* 1.15.

7. Socrates, *Ecclesiastical History* 1.6.

8. Sozomen, *Ecclesiastical History* 1.15.

9. Socrates, *Ecclesiastical History* 1.6.

10. Theodoret, *Ecclesiastical History* 1.5.

11. Athanasius, *On the Synods of Ariminium and Seleucia.*

12. Lewis Ayres, *Nicaea and Its Legacy: An Approach to Fourth-Century Trinitarian Theology* (New York: Oxford University Press, 2006), 52.

13. Rod Bennett, *The Apostasy That Wasn't* (El Cajon, CA: Catholic Answers, 2015), 109f.

14. Eusebius, *Church History* 10.9.6–7. I am not exaggerating about the blue skies and production numbers.

15. Eusebius, *Life of Constantine* 2.56.

16. Eusebius, *Life of Constantine* 2.63–72; see also Socrates, *Ecclesiastical History* 1.7.

17. Sozomen, *Ecclesiastical History* 1.17.

18. See Bennett, *The Apostasy That Wasn't*, 124.

19. Socrates, *Ecclesiastical History* 1.8.

20. Eusebius of Caesarea, *Letter to His Diocese*, 15.

21. Eusebius of Caesarea, *Letter to His Diocese*, 15.

22. Socrates, *Ecclesiastical History* 1.9.

23. Theodoret, *Ecclesiastical History* 1.19.

Chapter 4. The Empire Christianized

1. Socrates, *Ecclesiastical History* 1.26.

2. Socrates, *Ecclesiastical History* 1.14.

3. Eusebius, *Life of Constantine* 2.56.

4. Athanasius, *Apology against the Arians* 2.59.

Chapter 5. Pope Constantius

1. Julian, *Letter to the Athenians*, quoted in Adrian Murdoch, *The Last Pagan: Julian the Apostate and the Death of the Ancient World* (Rochester, VT: Inner Traditions, 2008), 14–15.

2. Socrates, *Ecclesiastical History* 2.3.

3. Socrates, *Ecclesiastical History* 2.3.

4. Bennett, *The Apostasy That Wasn't*, 189–90.

5. Socrates, *Ecclesiastical History* 1.37.

6. Socrates, *Ecclesiastical History* 1.37.

7. See Timothy S. Miller, *The Birth of the Hospital in the Byzantine Empire* (Baltimore: Johns Hopkins University Press, 1997), 76–84.

8. Philostorgius, *Ecclesiastical History* 2.5.

9. Theodoret, *Ecclesiastical History* 4.37.

10. Athanasius, *Apology against the Arians* 1.35.

11. Athanasius, *Apology against the Arians* 1.35.

12. Athanasius, *Apology against the Arians* 1.35.

13. Ammianus Marcellinus, *Res Gestae* 21.16.18.

14. Ammianus Marcellinus, *Res Gestae* 21.16.18.

15. Sulpicius Severus, *Chronica* 2.38.4–7.

16. *Theodosian Code* 16.10.3.

17. Ammianus Marcellinus, *Res Gestae* 22.5.

18. Athanasius, *History of the Arians* 4.33.

19. Athanasius, *Apologia for His Flight* 24–25.

20. Julian, *Letters* 23, quoted in Murdoch, *The Last Pagan*, 18.

Chapter 6. The Counterrevolution

1. Julian, *Misopogon* 361D–362B.

2. See Murdoch, *The Last Pagan*, 26–27.

3. Lucian, *On the Syrian Goddess* 50.

4. Bennett, *The Apostasy That Wasn't*, 235.

5. Murdoch, *The Last Pagan*, 134–35.

6. See Murdoch, *The Last Pagan*, 136.

7. Julian, *Letter to Artabius*.

8. Julian, *Letters* 22.

9. In his satire, the *Misopogon*.

10. In his satire, the *Misopogon*.

11. Julian, *Letters* 22.
12. Julian, *Letters* 22.

Chapter 7. The Christian Empire and Beyond

1. Gregory Nazianzen, *Orations*, 43.63.
2. Basil, *The Longer Rule*, question 7.
3. Basil, *The Longer Rule*, question 7.
4. Gregory of Nyssa, *Life of St. Macrina.*
5. Gregory of Nyssa, *Life of St. Macrina.*
6. Andrew T. Crislip, *From Monastery to Hospital: Christian Monasticism and the Transformation of Health Care in Late Antiquity* (Ann Arbor: University of Michigan Press, 2005), 60–67.
7. Quoted in Guenter B. Risse, *Mending Bodies, Saving Souls: A History of Hospitals* (New York: Oxford University Press, 1999), 76.
8. Theodoret, *Ecclesiastical History* 4.19.
9. Sozomen, *Ecclesiastical History* 3.15.
10. Ambrose, quoted in Murdoch, *The Last Pagan*, 27.
11. Gregory Nazianzen, *Orations* 42.24.

Chapter 8. A Tale of Two Bishops

1. Paulinus, *Life of Ambrose*, 6.
2. Ambrose, *Letters* 18.
3. Ambrose, *Letters* 20.
4. Adrian Murdoch, *The Last Roman: Romulus Augustulus and the Decline of the West* (Stroud, U.K.: Sutton, 2006), 29.
5. Ambrose, *Letters* 51.
6. Ambrose, *Letters* 51.
7. Ambrose, *Letters* 51.
8. John Chrysostom, *Homilies on the Statues* 13. 1.
9. Theodoret, *Ecclesiastical History* 5.19, and John Chrysostom, *Homilies on the Statues* 17.1. I've put these two sources together to make up Macedonius's speech, since they clearly narrate the same incident, although St. John Chrysostom does not name the monk.
10. Theodoret, *Ecclesiastical History* 5.19.
11. Socrates, *Ecclesiastical History* 6.18.

Chapter 9. An Age of Titans

1. *Theodosian Code* 16.5.6.
2. Libanius, *Pro Templis* 8.9.

3. Jerome, *Letters* 22.30.

4. Palladius, *Lausiac History* 36.6–7.

5. Jerome, *Letters* 45.

6. Jerome, *Letters* 127.

7. Jerome, *Letters* 127.7.

8. Jerome, *Preface to the Four Gospels*.

9. Augustine, *Confessions* 3.5.9.

Chapter 10. Decline and Fall

1. Jerome, *Letters* 127.12. Some of Jerome's strong language was suppressed by Victorian translators. It has been restored here.

2. Augustine, *City of God* 1.7.

3. Jerome, *Letters* 127.13.

4. Socrates, *Ecclesiastical History* 7.32.8.

5. Socrates, *Ecclesiastical History* 7.32.1–3, 9–10.

6. Socrates, *Ecclesiastical History* 7.15.6.

7. Cyril of Alexandria, *Letters* 4.

8. See Celestine, *Letters* 11.4.

9. See Cyril of Alexandria, *Letters* 17.

10. Nestorius, *The Book of Heracleides*.

Chapter 11. A Lamp in the Twilight

1. Augustine, *Letters* 228.14.

2. Salvian, *On the Government of God* 5.4.

3. Sulpicius Severus, *Life of St. Martin* 10.6.

4. Theodoret, *Letters* 113.

For Further Reading

Khaled Anatolios, *Retrieving Nicaea: The Development and Meaning of Trinitarian Doctrine* (Grand Rapids, MI: Baker, 2011).

Lewis Ayres, *Nicaea and Its Legacy: An Approach to Fourth-Century Trinitarian Theology* (New York: Oxford University Press, 2006).

Louis Bouyer et al., *The Spirituality of the New Testament and the Fathers*, vol. 1 in A History of Christian Spirituality (New York: Seabury, 1963).

William Harmless, *Desert Christians: An Introduction to the Literature of Early Monasticism* (Oxford: Oxford University Press, 2004).

Stephen M. Hildebrand, *Basil of Caesarea* (Grand Rapids, MI: Baker, 2014).

Richard M. Hogan, *Dissent from the Creed: Heresies Past and Present* (Huntington, IN: Our Sunday Visitor, 2001).

J. N. D. Kelly, *Golden Mouth: The Story of John Chrysostom, Ascetic, Preacher, Bishop* (Grand Rapids, MI: Baker, 1995).

Peter J. Leithart, *Defending Constantine: The Twilight of an Empire and the Dawn of Christendom* (Downers Grove, IL: IVP Academic, 2010).

Enrico Mazza, *Mystagogy: A Theology of Liturgy in the Patristic Age* (New York: Pueblo, 1989).

Adrian Murdoch, *The Last Pagan: Julian the Apostate and the Death of the Ancient World* (Rochester, VT: Inner Traditions, 2008).

John Henry Newman, *Arians of the Fourth Century* (Notre Dame, IN: University of Notre Dame Press, 2001).

———, *The Church of the Fathers* (Notre Dame, IN: University of Notre Dame Press, 2002).

———, *An Essay on the Development of Christian Doctrine* (Notre Dame, IN: University of Notre Dame Press, 1989).

John J. O'Meara, *The Young Augustine* (Staten Island, NY: Alba House, 2001).

Jaroslav Pelikan, *The Emergence of the Catholic Tradition (100–600),* vol. 1 in The Christian Tradition (Chicago: University of Chicago Press, 1971).

Joan M. Petersen, ed. and trans., *Handmaids of the Lord: Holy Women in Late Antiquity and the Early Middle Ages* (Kalamazoo, MI: Cistercian Publications, 1996).

David Potter, *Constantine the Emperor* (New York: Oxford University Press, 2012).

Philip Rousseau, *Basil of Caesarea* (Berkeley, CA: University of California Press, 1994).

Christoph Schönborn, *God Sent His Son: A Contemporary Christology* (San Francisco, CA: Ignatius Press, 2010).

Rodney Stark, *The Rise of Christianity: How the Obscure, Marginal Jesus Movement Became the Dominant Religious Force in the Western World in a Few Centuries* (San Francisco: HarperCollins, 1997).

J. Stevenson (revised by W. H. C. Frend), *Creeds, Councils, and Controversies: Documents Illustrating the History of the Church, AD 337–461* (London: SPCK, 1989).

Thomas G. Weinandy, *Athanasius: A Theological Introduction* (Washington, DC: Catholic University of America Press, 2018).

Robert Louis Wilken, *The First Thousand Years: A Global History of Christianity* (New Haven: Yale University Press, 2013).

———, *The Spirit of Early Christian Thought: Seeking the Face of God* (New Haven: Yale University Press, 2005).

Index

Mike Aquilina is a Catholic author, popular speaker, poet, and so[...] who serves as the executive vice president of the St. Paul Center f[...] cal Theology. He is a contributing editor to Angelus News.

Aquilina is the author or editor of more than fifty books, incl[...] *The Fathers of the Church*, *The Mass of the Early Christians*, and *A[...] of God*. He contributed work on early Christianity to the *Encyclopedi[...] Catholic Social Thought*. Aquilina has cohosted eleven series on EW[...] and hosted two documentaries. Aquilina wrote the companion volum[...] to the NBC miniseries *A.D.: The Bible Continues* (2015), and the MGN[...] remake of the movie *Ben-Hur* (2016). His book *A History of the Church in 100 Objects* earned an honorable mention in the 2018 Catholic Press Association awards.

He has published hundreds of articles, essays, and reviews in periodicals such as *First Things*, *Crisis*, *National Catholic Register*, *The Priest*, *Columbia*, and *Our Sunday Visitor*. He is a frequent guest on TV and radio, including a weekly appearance on the *Son Rise Morning Show*.

Aquilina previously served as editor of *New Covenant* magazine and *The Pittsburgh Catholic*. He has received honors from the Catholic Press Association, including "Best Magazine" for *New Covenant* during his editorship.

He lives in the Pittsburgh, Pennsylvania, area with his wife, Terri. They have six children.

Fathersofthechurch.com
Facebook: AuthorMikeAquilina

Reclaiming
...LIC HISTORY SERIES

The history of the Catholic Church
is often clouded by myth,
misinformation, and missing pieces.
Today there is a renewed interest
in recovering the true history
of the Church, correcting the record
in the wake of centuries
of half-truths and noble lies.
Books in the Reclaiming Catholic
History series, edited by Mike Aquilina
and written by leading authors and
historians, bring Church history to life,
debunking the myths one era at a time.

Titles in the Series Include:

The Early Church

*The Church and
the Roman Empire*

*The Church and
the Dark Ages*

*The Church and
the Middle Ages*

*The Church and
the Reformation*

*The Church and the Age
of Enlightenment*

*The Church Facing
the Modern Age*

**Look for titles in this series wherever books and eBooks are sold.
Visit avemariapress.com for more information.**

Mike Aquilina is a Catholic author, popular speaker, poet, and songwriter who serves as the executive vice president of the St. Paul Center for Biblical Theology. He is a contributing editor to Angelus News.

Aquilina is the author or editor of more than fifty books, including *The Fathers of the Church*, *The Mass of the Early Christians*, and *Angels of God*. He contributed work on early Christianity to the *Encyclopedia of Catholic Social Thought*. Aquilina has cohosted eleven series on EWTN and hosted two documentaries. Aquilina wrote the companion volumes to the NBC miniseries *A.D.: The Bible Continues* (2015), and the MGM remake of the movie *Ben-Hur* (2016). His book *A History of the Church in 100 Objects* earned an honorable mention in the 2018 Catholic Press Association awards.

He has published hundreds of articles, essays, and reviews in periodicals such as *First Things*, *Crisis*, *National Catholic Register*, *The Priest*, *Columbia*, and *Our Sunday Visitor*. He is a frequent guest on TV and radio, including a weekly appearance on the *Son Rise Morning Show*.

Aquilina previously served as editor of *New Covenant* magazine and *The Pittsburgh Catholic*. He has received honors from the Catholic Press Association, including "Best Magazine" for *New Covenant* during his editorship.

He lives in the Pittsburgh, Pennsylvania, area with his wife, Terri. They have six children.

Fathersofthechurch.com
Facebook: AuthorMikeAquilina